Character Sells

DEVELOPING THE TRAITS YOU NEED TO SUCCEED

MARK WILLIAMS

Character Sells, Developing the Traits You Need to Succeed

ISBN: 978-1-966382-81-2

Cover design: Mark Williams
Illustrations: Illustrations created through Microsoft Copilot

Published by EABooks Publishing, a division of
Living Parables of Central Florida, Inc. a 501c3

EABooksPublishing.com

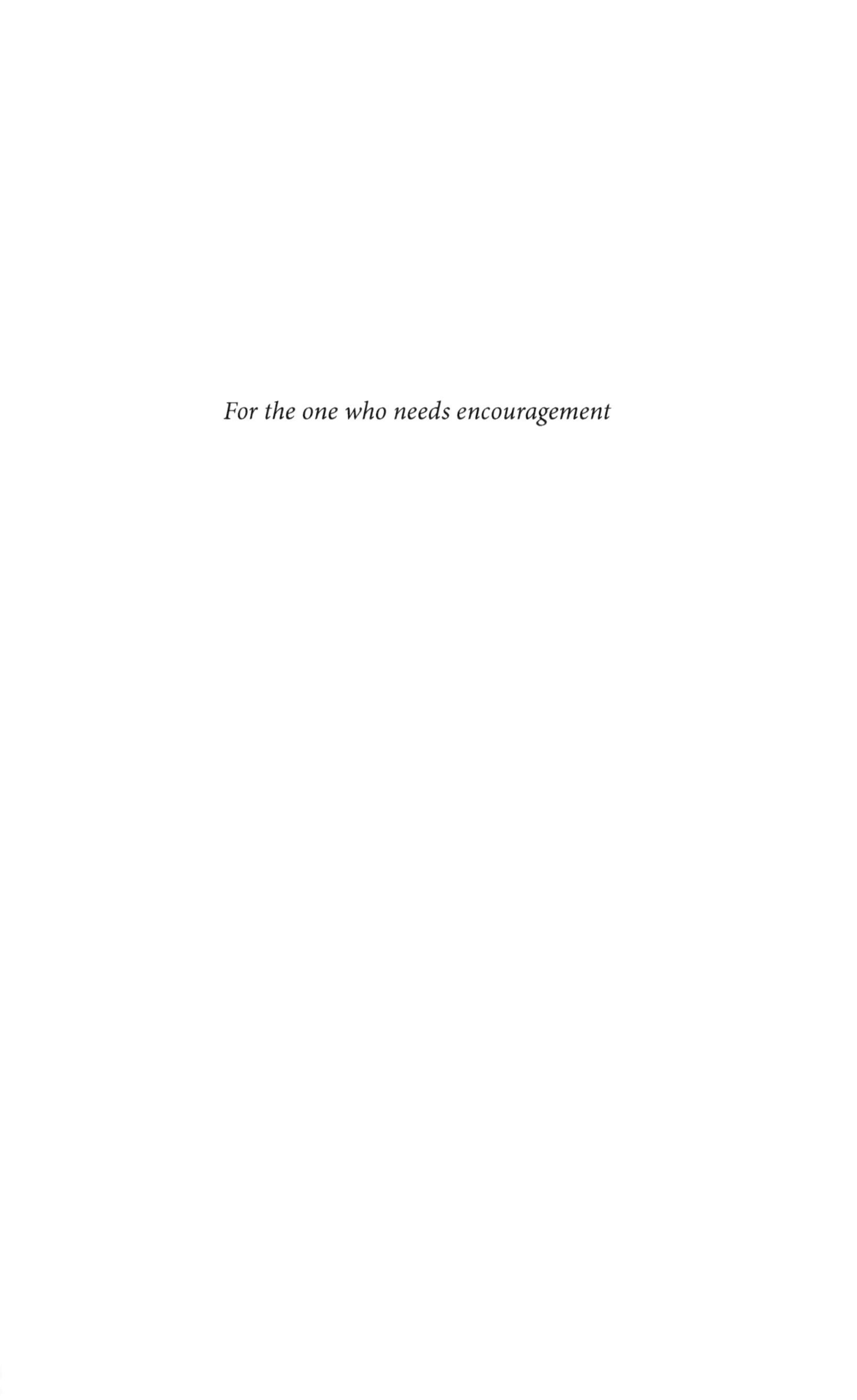

For the one who needs encouragement

Sell: to persuade or influence
to a course of action
or the acceptance of something.[1]
—Merriam-Webster Dictionary

Contents

Getting Started

In 1792 a gentleman from Virginia by the name of Adam O'Brien made his way to the center of West Virginia and settled there. Over the years many others followed him, including John D. Sutton, after whom the town was eventually named. Located at the very center of the state formed in 1863, it is the county seat for Braxton County, named after Carter Braxton, who was one of the signers of the Declaration of Independence. Sutton's centrality in the region and access to the Elk River made it a viable access point for major transportation routes. Unfortunately, during the Civil War most of the town was burned to the ground. After the war rebuilding slowly commenced. And to this day, Sutton remains a small historic little town.

Throughout our lives we live and move through places that have seen history like this. Sometimes we are simply onlookers at the remnants of stories from what was. Other times, without even realizing it, a place that was once significant to someone else may hold some future significance for us as well. Sutton is one of those places for me.

The first time I drove through Sutton, I had been working for my family business, which manages hotels around the country. In 2013 our company received a lead to manage a hotel near Sutton. I flew from Orlando to Charlotte and made the trek north toward the East River Mountain Tunnel that leads into West Virginia.

There are passageways around the world where you go through a tunnel or cross a bridge, and it feels as if you have left one realm and entered another. The East River Mountain Tunnel is one of those places. Accessibility is not a word you would use to describe getting to and from central West Virginia. Its remoteness contributes to its slogan of being "Wild and Wonderful." Early settlers like Adam O'Brien must have recognized this as they settled areas throughout the Appalachian Mountains.

The lead I was following came from one of our hotel franchise partners. This is a common occurrence in the hotel industry. Brand representatives will often reach out to management groups in whom they have confidence. Sometimes it is on behalf of owners who are seeking operational assistance. In other circumstances they may see a need for help from the outside that owners cannot see from the inside. As people become familiar and close to their normal environment, they can miss out on details that contribute to the overall impression of an experience or answer to a problem. Fresh eyes tend to brighten the dark cloudy areas of situations that contain opportunities and solutions waiting to be found.

Leads and referrals from those who have confidence in you and your company help provide sustainability. This applies to many products or experiences we purchase in life. Think about when you go out to eat. You are probably more likely to try a location that a trusted friend recommends versus some place you've never been before. Over the years I have had many people who have needed assistance send references to our company and me. A number of those referrals turned into significant business for us.

During the time we were working on this project in West Virginia, we traveled all over different pockets of the country. We would look at and review any project, whether it was big or small. This property was one of those small opportunities. Yet for us at this point, we were operating from the mindset of pulling in every piece of business possible. I spent my time on this visit with the franchise operations representative, getting a better understanding of the property and the location. This individual also provided me with a better picture of the ownership group I would be speaking with. Before leaving the area, I charted a time to return when I would present our company and services to the ownership group. I would be selling them on who we are and what we could do for them. Like Adam O'Brien many years before me, I would seek to establish something new. Not a new town or settlement but rather a new partnership.

What often ends up happening in sales and business is not always the monetary gain that we realize. It's growth—growth for our companies and business in terms of scale and reach. However, it is more than that. It is growth for us personally. With each passing experience, we have the opportunity to grow ourselves with fresh perspectives and knowledge. And as time moves along, we grow in greater understanding of how to better respond to the world around and within us. That is, of course, if we take the moments we are given and seek to gain the most from them.

If we are intentional about growing ourselves personally, we will ultimately strengthen the traits we want to see flourish within. What is grown and developed inside us will eventually be produced outside of us. This is called bearing fruit. And these traits make up our character. In Scripture the apostle Paul talks about this when he is writing to the church in Colossae. In Colossians chapter 1, verse 10, he says they are praying for them, "so that you may walk worthy of the Lord, fully pleasing to him: bearing fruit in every good work." I believe bearing fruit in every good work is something we all desire. This starts with cultivating great character traits within.

At the end of the day, character—strong character—is what truly sells.

After this initial visit I was confident that upon my return to central West Virginia, I would emerge victorious. While victories do indeed occur to us all, they may not necessarily happen the way we have initially mapped them out in our mind. The adaptive experiences of both victory and defeat help shape us to be better. They build a history within us that is more resilient, encouraged, and confident for whatever the future holds.

So, where does a journey begin for those who seek to shape themselves better? How does one become more effective at selling and seeing their dreams become reality? How do we develop character traits we want to grow, and others want to see?

If you are unsure, like I have been, let us at least take the first step forward in the words of Mark Twain, who said, "The secret of getting ahead is getting started."[1]

CHAPTER 1

What You Need

I never met a ragged boy in the street without feeling
that I may owe him a salute,
for I know not what possibilities may be buttoned up under his coat.
—James A. Garfield

I suspect that the lens through which you have been viewing your life may be a bit blurred. I know because I have looked through the same glasses as well. Your occupation may be that of a nurse, student, artist, delivery driver, construction worker, teacher, president of a division, or a dolphin trainer. However, the truth is you are actually first and foremost a salesperson.

Everyone, no matter who they are or where they are from, is in sales.

If you have worked for a business, whether directly in the sales department or not, you have been part of the sales team.

Does this surprise you?

It is true, though, whether you realize it or not, you are contributing to make that business function and hopefully be successful. It does not matter if you're restocking shelves, waiting tables, inputting data, driving a truck, or playing a banjo in a corner, you are indirectly or directly assisting with the selling of a product or service. That's because collectively with your fellow teammates you help create an impression or an experience for the customers your business touches. That touch point, from a business standpoint, hopefully triggers a response in the mind of the guest or customer for them to want to return.

It does not have to be a traditional business in the way you may be thinking. It could be a non-profit, church, hospital, committee, association, or lemonade stand.

Having said this, everyone being in sales is not just about being a contributing part of a company, business, or team. It's also about us individually. The truth is that we sell ourselves each day to the people in our spheres of influence. We sell our personality and presence to friends, family members, co-workers, neighbors, and even familiar faces we bump into at the grocery store. When done in the right way, people want to be around us. They will be less resistant to what we may be selling and more inclined to hear what we have to say.

Beyond being more captivating, there may be moments where we outwardly seek to sell an idea, dream, or passion. You never know whom you may come across today or tomorrow to help make that happen. We may be one faithful step away from another human being in the world who might assist in making our dreams become a reality. How well we sell ourselves in those opportune moments has the potential to breathe life into our ideas and passions. Why? Because *you* are the person behind it.

Have you ever dined in or heard of Rainforest Café?

Steve Schussler, the founder of the restaurant chain, became passionate about the tropical rainforest at an early age. He eventually had a dream of creating a restaurant where guests would have a dining experience that would be both educational and immersive. Schussler went to great lengths to sell others on his dream by converting his home into a replica of what a future Rainforest Café could look like. In the end it took him three years and roughly four hundred thousand dollars to get his home to a place that was ready to show to investors. Through a lot of persistence, he was able to finally get an investor named Lyle Berman to back him on the dream. Over the course of two years, Berman made over twenty visits to Schussler's house without any commitment.

According to Schussler, "When you're passionate about what you are doing, you'll do whatever needs to be done to reach your objective, to attain your goal. Failure isn't an option, the word 'no' isn't in your vocabulary."[1] If it were any other person besides Schussler selling the dream of having a restaurant that looks like a humid tropical rainforest it may very well never have been realized. It is the person and their passion that collectively makes improbable opportunities possible. Lyle Berman didn't just eventually become sold on the idea; he became sold on Schussler the person as well.

This book does not focus solely on the framework of business and how we can sell products and services better. There are plenty of resources that will help strengthen a person's techniques and performance in the art of selling. There is nothing wrong with sharpening the tools of closing lines and negotiation tactics. I believe the stories and learning lessons shared will help with all of that. However, the goal of this book is to focus on you. Regardless of whether you work for a company or not, whether you are growing up or are retired, no matter if you are looking to make a dream come to life or someone else's life better, I want you to be able to sell yourself in an impactful way. Selling yourself effectively will enhance the relationships that you have. It will open more doors for opportunities to connect with others. It will lead to greater success whether you are part of a sales team of one or many. It may even take the direction of your life down avenues you did not think you would explore and to heights you did not think you were able to reach.

Remember, what you are really selling is what people want to buy: trust and confidence in you.

Having confidence in something or someone is amazing. It's kind of like giving a trusted friend or relative the keys to your home while you leave to go away on a trip. You can trust that your home will be taken care of because you believe that person is reliable.

It does not matter if you are starting from square one in whatever industry you are in. It does not matter if you are a veteran pro who is a master of your craft. It does not matter if you scribbled an idea on a note pad in the middle of the night and you are excited to share it with someone. As a salesperson, the goal is to always cultivate reliability and trust. That reliability you build extends into the products, services, dreams, and ideas you sell. As we will see in the pages ahead, it does not matter if you wear the highest-priced outfit to your next sales meeting. You do not need an expensive suit to make the sale. Those faces in front of you cannot see the price tags or brand names hidden behind the stitching. However, it does not take long for people to see the real you.

Make sure you wear the real you on the outside. People will eventually see it. Be authentic. Nurture the character traits that you desire to grow.

When I was a kid, my mom had a picture of Georges Seurat's famous painting *A Sunday Afternoon on the Island of Grande Jatte* hanging in our basement. We had a nicely framed copy. The original painting was done in what is called pointillist technique. The whole painting is comprised of tiny individually colored dots. When you step back, all the dots look connected together as one complete picture. That technique is like the way character traits work. When people step back and see you, they see the comprehensive portrait of your individual character traits come to life as one. When they get closer to you, those individual character traits become distinguishable.

The goal of these pages is to help trigger thoughts that may lead to ways you can positively build on the mosaic of your character. In turn, the character you build will filter into that genuine and authentic you that people grow to see clearly and trust. The hope is that when you look back some distance in time from now, you will reflect on the steps you have taken with appreciation. You will thank yourself for allocating moments to learn and become more effective at selling who you are.

Why?

Because you matter. You really matter. Do you believe that? You have something in you waiting to be shared that can make the world better or someone else's world brighter. What if for that someone else, a significant moment for them was the day you crossed paths in their life? A day where you were not just a spectator but an active participant who helped foster success and significance.

Wouldn't that be amazing?

Where I'm Coming From

Most of my life and career has been within the hospitality industry. I have found that many roads lead back to hospitality no matter what you do and where you go. My wife was going to be a music major, and I was going to be a theater major. Despite our different paths, we both found hospitality, and we're glad we did. The care and provision for weary travelers and people in general became part of the business model centuries ago. People and businesses benefit from the fundamentals of service and skillfully caring for others. When company cultures are infused with heartfelt customer service and guest-centric thinking, it usually leads to positive outcomes. Though it is important to note that when I say, "guest," I am referring to both internal and external ones. This includes both the team members that work with you or for you and the customers that buy from you. The care and concern for your internal team are just as important, if not more so, than for your external customers and guests. Remember this motto from a speaker named Steve Gilliand: "If you take care of people, the business will follow."[2] The level of internal love and care you pour into yourself, and your team will yield immeasurable results externally.

Hospitality is a broad industry in terms of the number of business segments it reaches. You can go from operating theme park attractions all the way across the spectrum to senior living care. My focus is specifically on hotels and managing different types of lodging establishments. Even more challenging than managing hotels is the art of tactfully managing the people working inside them. It is not easy. If it were, then everyone would do it!

While the hotel business sandbox may seem friendly on the surface, the industry itself is one of the most competitive arenas in the global marketplace. My grandfather and his partner started our family business back in 1961. They initially focused on construction, and in 1971 they started building and owning hotels. Since that time, hundreds of competitors have risen to eat up more slices of the overall pie. People outside of hospitality tend to think that top hotels chains like Marriott and Hilton own and run all their locations. That is not the case. While franchises manage some of the buildings that bear their names, most do not. They are continuing to get further away from this model. Thus, the reliance on skilled and effective hotel operators has become increasingly prevalent.

Today numerous owners and operators manage their own properties. While a lot of consolidation has occurred, across the world there are still countless small, large, and mega management groups. Each of these companies essentially performs the same or similar functions. Yet it is how the functions are performed that creates large distinctions between them all. Performance and corresponding results (whether good, bad, or okay) are the culmination of the character and culture fostered by each respective workplace. The same is true for each respective person. The traits you nourish determine the eventual health of the fruit that is produced.

Matthew records the words of Jesus when he says, "Either make the tree good and its fruit good or make the tree bad and its fruit bad; the tree is recognized and judged by its fruit." (Matthew 12:33). He continues in verse 35 by saying, "A good person produces good things from his storeroom of good." What you put in is what you will get out when it comes to company culture and personal character. Let's seek to make deposits into our storeroom of good character so that we can produce good as a result.

Having been in and around hospitality for most of my life, I have had the opportunity to experience a lot of positives and negatives. It is an industry that is generally, among peers, very welcoming and receptive to helping one another. I will never forget the people along my career journey who took it upon themselves to willingly offer up their time to be a resource. One such person was Jim Knight who was the former Director of Training for Hard Rock Cafe. Knight was gracious enough to have my wife and me come and tour the Hard Rock offices many years ago. He willingly gave us thoughts and advice on how to put together rock star material for our company. It was great.

Experiences like this with Knight and many others have in turn oriented me toward giving myself to others when I can. It is truly awesome to be around people who expect nothing in return. Whenever and wherever possible we should seek to be givers and not takers.

On the flip side of all this, I have seen things over the years that were cutthroat between people and organizations. The disgust you feel emotionally is palpable. Experiences on the dark side of the moon of business and relationships are not pleasant and not what anyone wants. However, challenging situations and difficult people are woven into the fabric of the world. While we cannot avoid them, we can embrace both the good and bad to make us stronger and wiser for the journey ahead.

One of the biggest challenges I think we face is being joyful in the dark periods just as much as the bright and easy ones. It is important to find joy in whatever you do and wherever you find yourself. If joyfulness is imbedded within you, you'll have greater stability no matter the terrain you find yourself walking through.

Most of my career in hospitality has been working within the department of business development. It is a unique position and at its core, business development is all about selling what we do for owners who may be seeking to change their operator. There are other situations such as when owners who are buying a hotel need someone to run it. One of the amazing aspects of sales and business development that I have loved is seeing ideas come to life. I love dreams that originate from collaborative discussions and brainstorms that can eventually turn into something real. What may have been a thought one day in the past can eventually transform into an actual building, project, or program tomorrow. What I love most, though, is the opportunities that can be created for others.

Do you ever view selling that way? The efforts you make not only create opportunities for yourself, but they also create opportunities for others.

Where does it all start? It begins with you and your team believing in the knowledge, skills, and abilities you have developed. From there it is taking those daily steps of faith through calls and conversation to build bridges to relationships.

Life really is a journey. I am not done growing and becoming the best salesperson I can be.

Nor are you.

Don't quit. Keep moving.

Debrief

Quite often after a sales call, presentation, contract signing, or the termination of an agreement, our team and I would take the time to debrief. From the experiences we encounter it's important to take a moment to reflect and note what worked and what did not. Take mental and physical notes of the goods, the bads, and the uglies. What do you want to start doing, stop doing and keep doing? If you worked together with other team members, I encourage you to take time to debrief with them, even if it's just a quick phone call. Whenever you can, take time to acknowledge with another team member or friend how each of you felt about what happened. If it is just yourself, take mental and physical notes of what did and did not work.

Even if you have been selling your product for many years, you should never want to stop learning. We should always be willing to grow, adapt, and listen. This way we will be able to stay dialed in to customer preferences and trends. Beyond that, we will be able to keep a better finger on the pulse of social interactions. We will become better at pivoting in conversations, knowing when to speak and when to listen. We will be able to change the way we present and share information, so it becomes more refined and smoother in the delivery.

Ideas

Join a Group

There is a season for everything. It may not always be possible with the schedule that you have. When you can, join a committee or working group. Becoming part of a smaller team working together on a project helps create relationships in your industry, community, and company. Solving problems together builds friendships and connections that may come in handy down the road. So often in life things are about whom you know. Over the years I have been a part of different boards, committees, and working groups. I am thankful for the connections that were made by being a part of them. You will be thankful as well.

Sales Tracking

A critical piece for sales is having a tracking system for all leads that you come across. A platform for storing contact information, conversations, notes, reminders, and times to follow up. Keep track of your sales leads or traces with a system that works for you. I once talked to someone who used sticky notes to keep track of everything. I never knew how they were able to do that, but it worked for them. Today we have all kinds of applications and cloud-based solutions available. My system has been a combination of using a journal I can make notes in paired with a cloud-based system for storing information. Implement a system that works best for you.

Say Thanks

I am guilty of not doing a better job with this one. Writing handwritten thank-you notes has become a lost art. When you can, take time to send a thank-you note to the prospects and clients you are working with. Take time to say thanks to the team members or great vendor relationships you work with. Few people do this, and when you do, it will leave a lasting positive impression. Thank people for their time, thank them for their business, thank them for the opportunity to work together. There are endless ways to express gratitude.

Questions to Consider

- Do a quick search online for "attributes of a strong character." What character trait do you think people see in you the most? Is there one or more you feel needs to be nurtured and grown further?
- What do you love most about what you do now?
- There may be someone you would like to ask for advice and help. Who is that person? When will you ask them?
- Is there someone you know whom you can spend time with to help them grow?

We may affirm absolutely that nothing great in the world has been accomplished without passion.

—G. W. F. Hegel, *The Great Bridge Book*

Your Takeaways

What are some initial impressions that stood out to you from this first chapter? What do you want to remember and bring with you down the road ahead? ______________________________

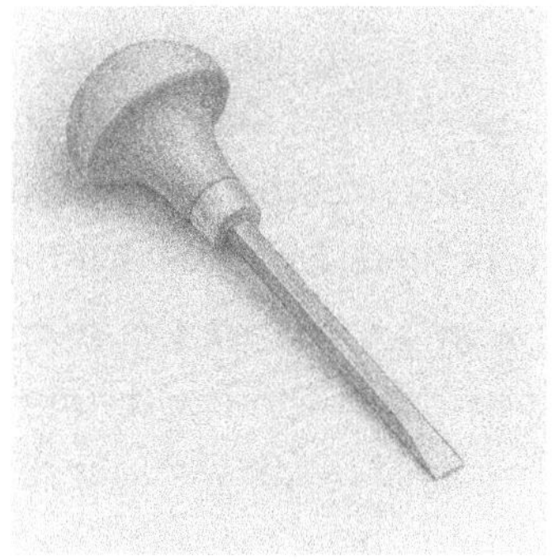

CHAPTER 2

The Most Important Thing You Sell

Don't be distracted by criticism.
Remember, the only taste of success some people get
is to take a bite out of you.
—Zig Ziglar

The time came for me once again to head back to Sutton, West Virginia, to see the property we were bidding to manage. I wanted to study the market further, review the hotel and its competition, and hopefully convince the ownership group to let us manage their asset. Giving yourself extra time to gain a better understanding of your customers and their situation is helpful. The more knowledge and information you have stored away in your mind prior to the initial meeting the better. First impressions are very important. During that initial in-person or virtual meeting, you're more apt to speak intelligently about questions and comments that may arise. Given the size of the general area and the smaller number of competitors, it did not take a lot of time for me to complete a review of the market.

For being a small seventy-four-room hotel in a little town, there was a large group of about six representatives that made up the ownership entity of this property. Over the years I've seen that having multiple voices in a partnership can lead to potential conflict and disagreement. However, most of them agreed in this instance that they needed to hire a third-party operator to manage the property. A lot of investors do not want to get into the day-to-day management of a hotel. That is part of the reason why hotel management companies exist.

As was typical, I studied and prepared everything the day before the meeting. Also, as was typical, I brought my trusty, dark grey suit from a well-known apparel store so I would look professional. I cannot remember how much I paid for the suit, but it was not expensive. Every suit I had around this time was from that store and after many meetings and events; they had not failed me yet. But you cannot always plan when expiration dates happen on clothing. Unfortunately, late into the afternoon on this trip I noticed that the seam around my groin area was looking like it would become undone. Could this be the time the tried-and-true suit failed me now? The meeting with the owners was the following morning.

We have all had moments where we internally motivate and pump ourselves up. You have probably done this before a sporting match, a test, stepped onstage, or some other nerve-racking experience. This internal motivation is especially important before meeting a potential client. I cannot tell you how many times my father did this before he went into a meeting. He would find a bathroom outside the client's office, or we would be in the car on the way to the appointment together. My Dad would look at himself in the mirror and say, "I like myself! I'm a great salesman!" He did this repeatedly. Do it enough and you will find yourself going into the meeting pumped up, energetic, and believing that the prospective client will enjoy hearing what you have to say. If you do not believe me, give self-motivation a try sometime. There is power in words, especially ones you repetitively say to yourself.

With the suit being torn before the meeting, I tried to pump myself up with this situation like any other. I said to myself in the mirror, "You can fix this!" But I am not a tailor, and I have never really taken the time to sew anything ever in my life. If my life depended on it, I do not think I could manage proper stitches. So, I lied to myself when I said, "You can fix this!"

After calling my wife for some directions and encouragement, I really did feel that I could make it happen in this situation. Besides, I was in the middle of West Virginia, the sun was beginning to set over the mountains, and my meeting was the next morning. There would be no time to find another suit. And being the semi-frugal person that I am, why would I want to spend money on a new outfit when I could repair the suit I already had? Since I did not have a sewing kit on me, I navigated my way to a nearby drug store that happened to have one for sale. That evening, I sewed up the hole and matched the thread as best I could. Problem solved! Right?

The next morning dressed and ready to go, I left the hotel to get coffee. I just needed to finish setting up the meeting room before doing my presentation. Always make sure to leave enough time to test your tech before a presentation. By the time I got back to the property, what was previously a clear sky had turned dark and formidable. The heavens eventually opened into a torrential downpour. It was raining so hard there was no way I would avoid getting wet on my way to the hotel lobby. The internal motivator kicked in: "You can do this! You will be dry in no time before the meeting starts." On the count of three I would make a break for the hotel. One. Two. Three. Go! As I thrust open the driver's side door and turned on the seat, the pants were what made the break for it. Yes, my poorly stitched seam came undone, and the little opening in the crotch area became a gaping hole.

Have you ever been in a moment when you felt helpless and could not do anything about your circumstances? This happens periodically, but it seems that it does more frequently when traveling. Over the years all sorts of mishaps have occurred when I was going from point A to B. I once left my computer at the airport terminal security and opened my bag on the plane only to find it was not there. On another plane ride I was sitting in my seat when someone took my bag, which was a couple rows ahead. I have been stuck in hours' worth of traffic, been lost, caught in snowstorms, and stood up by people I was supposed to meet. One time I was in Phoenix for a conference. After the event concluded and before leaving, I decided to climb up Squaw Peak near the city. I made it all the way to the top only to realize that the plane I was booked on was scheduled to leave in thirty minutes.

How we respond in moments when things do not go according to plan can be very defining. The ability to react, respond, pivot, and adjust in a meaningful way will shape outcomes in our lives either positively or negatively. Sometimes we make situations bigger than they are. If you pull yourself up and away from the moment, try to view what you are facing against a larger span of time. You can ask yourself: Is what I am facing going to matter one week from now, one year from now or ten years from now? In that moment pulling yourself back may help make what you are going thorough feel less overwhelming.

It is a guarantee in life that mishaps, surprises, and challenges will happen. This is typically where our freedom of choice comes into play. We can choose to respond with optimism, or we can choose to go down the path of negativity. I have always liked the saying "Two men looked out through prison bars. One saw mud and the other saw stars." It does not mean we always get it right. But we should strive to view circumstances in a different light.

For me at this hotel in West Virgina, miles from home, I did not have a lot of choices with my situation. Though this could be a very embarrassing moment, I knew I had to press on. Slightly soaked and with nowhere to escape, I made my way into the meeting room before everyone arrived. After assessing the damage, I figured that if I stayed seated with my legs under the table, I might be okay. If I had to stand up, I would just keep my legs as close together as possible. The clients started arriving, and at least four-to-five of them showed up. I did not turn my back on anyone the whole time. I kept my gaze locked on everyone and my legs at tight attention until I could slide into a chair. Thankfully, the presentation went well.

To this day I can only hope that no one saw the gaping hole or paid much attention to my rigid stance. After several follow-up exchanges, we signed a deal and started managing the property in 2014. The pants were not so fortunate.

One of the lessons I learned from this experience is that I did not need an expensive suit to make that sale or others I have made over the course of my career. You do need functional and professional attire. Yet getting people to buy your product or service is more than the way you look or dress. The name brand hidden on a swatch of fabric is something people cannot see anyway. Costly items that you wear on the outside of yourself are less important than the priceless attributes you develop within. The brand that should be most visibly seen is your character. This is true at any age and any stage in life. It is applicable if you are seeking a position or opportunity. Yet it is even truer when you seek to develop or foster any type of relationship. In either case you are first getting people to buy into you.

Honing the ability to effectively get buy-in from others is like creating and putting up a sales banner above yourself. That banner forms a strong representation of how people will feel about the product or service you're selling. Whether working with a company or not, one of the biggest things you will sell in life is yourself. And this is done by creating impressions on people.

There are two types of impressions you can leave on the individuals you come across. First impressions are typically formed within seven seconds of meeting someone. These are the ones that give people those gut feelings, during and after the meeting, about whether they want to go with you or not. Another saying goes that you never get a second chance to make a first impression. That's because the first ones may end up being the long-lasting ones that people never forget.

Deep-rooted impressions can take a lot longer because they are grown with seeds of trust. Trust takes time and effort. Trust takes care and consistency. Trust has the power to blossom into strong loyalty that can generate sales opportunities that would not happen in any other way.

In the end it is who you are, and the person you're intentionally becoming, that is more important than a physical product you're selling or what you're wearing. The character traits you're developing help make up the person you're becoming. The word *character* is derived from Greek and means a mark from an engraving tool, or to engrave. If you have ever taken a chisel to a piece of stone or a knife to a piece of wood, the mark that is left becomes permanent—unless you keep working on the material and keep engraving. If you reach a place where you feel that you have developed traits that are not leading to growth, do not stop engraving. Keeping working on making marks that refine you more toward the person you are seeking to be.

As we close out this chapter, remember, you do not need an expensive suit to make the sale. You do, however, need to believe in yourself. Wouldn't you agree that believing in the product you're selling gives you more confidence? The same is true for you. If you do not believe in *you*, you'll struggle to make connections and win. With confidence you can be ready to step into almost any sales situation. The most important thing we will ever sell to someone else is ourselves. Believe in and be honest with the person you are looking at on the other side of the mirror.

Put Guardrails Around the Framework of Your Business

We ended up realizing that the property I discussed in this chapter was too small and too far from the corporate office. It was not easily accessible because there was not a close enough airport to fly into. The property operations and sales teams providing support had to drive in from different directions. Coming from the office, this would take about four-and-a-half hours without traffic or weather delays. Cell phone coverage also got spotty on some parts of the trip.

As time progresses on projects, cumbersome travel creates fatigue for yourself and your team. Fatigue can lead to frustration. This is especially true when little is produced for all the work and effort. You and your team must also figure out what makes the most sense logistically for your business. The same is true with figuring out what makes the most sense logistically for yourself and your family.

It is important that a company and organization put a framework around the key elements of ideal target deals they feel are optimal for the business. If you are a part of the executive team with your company, you must collectively decide who you *are* and who you are *not*. Also decide which projects your team can be effective with and which ones they will not. If you are part of the business development team, it's important for you to understand this because it will shield your team from setting itself up for eventual failure. Do not just take in every piece of business you can get. Navigate the output that will be needed from the team to support the client. This includes evaluating the time, money, and resources needed to truly be successful.

But leave room for exceptions. With some projects you may need to sell your own company and team on why it is worth the risk. It may take time and experience to see these projects of opportunity when others do not. Remember the same applies for you personally. Seek to put guardrails around your life as well. This includes decisions about whom you associate with and where you allocate your time. Guard your heart. Proverbs 4:23 says, "Guard your heart above all else, for it is the source of life."

Outline Your Costs Clearly

After we had been managing the hotel for a little while, the owners of the property started to complain about the breakdown of the monthly invoices they were receiving. Most hotel management companies have a fee for service that is based off a percentage of revenue. This fee percentage has fluctuated over time, but typically it will be around 3 percent of total hotel revenue. There are also other fees or expenses that may be included, as well as pass-through costs to the hotel that the property must absorb. An example of this would be reimbursement for travel to the hotel or software costs. The owners of the hotel felt misled because they were seeing the additional pass-through costs of the statement. They felt we were not transparent and upfront with all the fees and expenses that were going to be charged. Their expectation was that all expenses from the management company would be rolled into the base management fee. While this is clearly not the case, the result of all this led to frustrated conversations and the eventual breakdown of the business relationship.

We had a list of all these expenses, but they were not all specifically spelled out in the hotel management agreement. This was a lesson for us. We learned from that point on the importance of outlining potential costs as clearly as possible. If a client is paying you or your company for a product or service, they should know clearly what their money is or is not getting them. Unfortunately, I have seen companies that have been disingenuous and not forthcoming about amounts on an invoice.

Not being transparent about reimbursable expenses can end up backfiring in a big way. It can cost a company future revenue, but more importantly, it can lead to trust and confidence being depleted. This isn't helpful when trust is what you are trying to grow. Remember that no company or business is perfect. From time-to-time mistakes can and will happen. The way you and your team respond when those mistakes happen will make all the difference in the world. Responding well to mistakes can put you in a better place in the minds of a guest or client than if the mistake had not happened in the first place.

When it comes to transparency, if you are selling your dream, project, or idea to someone else, try to be as mindful as you can about the costs. Costs are not just currency. They are also time, energy, and effort.

From that point on in our company's approach, we created a full exhibit in our management agreement to outline as many fees and extra costs as possible. The goal was to eliminate as many unknowns as possible and be transparent. We managed this property for a year and ended up parting ways. I have found that you can learn just as much from unsuccessful deals as you can from successful ones. Regardless of the deal or the result, be wise. You'll always find something to be learned or reminded of.

The Important Lesson of Leaving Room for Error

When you have actively scheduled time to present or sell (virtually or in person) make sure you give yourself extra time. If you are going to a specific destination, factor in extra travel time if you can. It is awful to be in a frenzied panic of being late for a meeting in a sales situation. I have been there many times. Mostly it is due to circumstances beyond our control, but adding a margin of time always helps.

Included with this is factoring extra time to test your tech in advance. While people can be understanding, it comes off as unprofessional if you are fumbling with getting internet, screens, and cords connected. If sounds and videos are supposed to play, then those should be tested in advance. Also pull up the documents you want to share in advance, so you are not searching for them among many files on your computer. It's okay to ask your prospective client if you can come a little early to set up the space they have set aside for you. You are setting yourself up for greater success if everything you have wanted to share and convey is running the way you intended. Always have backups and an extra notebook or paper printed. If you have saved something on your computer, make sure to save it on the cloud or a separate USB flash drive as well. These backups not only are inexpensive, but they also give you peace of mind.

Along the lines of leaving room for error is throwing in an extra back-up piece of clothing in your suitcase in case of emergency, like a ripped seam. Over the years I have had all types of food dropped and spilled on me. It has been everything from breakfast sausage grease spraying on my suit, chocolate on my pants, and coffee spilling everywhere. There is nothing like dropping a large hot coffee in your lap while driving on the interstate. You may be questioning whether I can eat and drink properly. The point is that accidents do happen. Expect the unexpected and plan accordingly.

Last, when I think about leaving room for error, this also means allowing room for grace. Be sure to give yourself grace and mercy for the mistakes that occur. You are learning and growing along with others that you encounter in life. Do not beat yourself up for things that happen outside of your control. Take the best lessons from those moments for next time, then keep laughing, smiling, and moving forward.

Take the Road Less Traveled

Over the years I have pursued business opportunities where many others would have initially walked away right off the bat. I have always believed that it is important in some cases to take those opportunities down the road a little bit so you can peak around the corner. Sometimes what may seemingly look like nothing can turn out to be something special.

Years ago, our company had been managing a great property near Dulles International Airport. The owner of that property liked what we were doing and asked my father if we would be able to manage a couple of other locations he owned. These properties were not in the greatest area nor were they in the greatest condition. We ended up passing on that opportunity. Sometime thereafter our client ended up tearing down those old properties and built two brand new hotels. He hired another group to manage them, who eventually took over the management of the great property we had by the airport.

By not going down the road a bit further, we allowed our competitor to get their foot in the door, and we missed out on significant fees for our company. We could have looked more at how the area was going to develop in the future. We could have sought to help our longstanding client with the projects they were looking to develop. Unfortunately, we lost a great business relationship. At least we learned a lesson.

You obviously must evaluate what is best for your business and yourself. Based upon your experiences and framework that has been established, you must know when to hold and fold. But be mindful of looking beyond the immediate.

One time we took a chance to manage some hotels in South Dakota near the base of Mt. Rushmore. It was a selling experience I will never forget. I got to eat rattlesnake, meet a guy named Lefty, and watch a magic show. The project would have been a unique opportunity, but the client ended up being the problem. I never want to shift blame, point fingers, or not take responsibility for our own actions. However, this group simply did not want to relinquish control and let us do the job we were hired to do. They would not get out of their own way.

That's also a lesson for being successful at selling in life. Sometimes we must be willing to get out of our own way. This takes humility, discernment, wise counsel, and patience. We want to get it right with timing when we act and when we do not. Getting it right can eliminate a lot of roadblocks on our paths toward achievement.

Overall, it has been my experience that most people do not typically keep the big picture in mind. They are quick to narrowly see the circumstances in front of them without looking beyond them. My encouragement is to take the road less traveled so you can at least see what is around the corner. What you may find could be incredibly impactful and positive for you and your company.

Ideas

First Impressions

As I mentioned in this chapter, you never get a second chance to make a first impression. Everything you read suggests that people form a first impression within the first few seconds of meeting you. That is extremely fast! While an expensive suit does not mean you will make the sale, looking presentable will help. Beyond what you are physically wearing, put on your real genuine self. Being the real, genuine, and authentic you will help leave a positive first impression that others will not forget.

Be Honest

Always seek to speak the truth even if it may cost you. The costs in the end will not be as much if you lie and are not upfront about mistakes and errors that are made. Gordon Ramsay, the famous British chef cannot stand lies. In his autobiography he speaks about the chefs he works with in the kitchen and when mistakes are made. Ramsay says, "The first thing we teach our chefs: not to lie. Even if it's born of panic, of a fear of getting into trouble, that doesn't change the fact that it's a great big lie."[1] He speaks to the fact that when someone lies, it breaks trust, and that trust takes years to rebuild if ever. As you seek to be successful at selling in life, be honest with yourself and with others.

Questions to Consider

- Think about some of the bigger purchases you've made in life and the people who made that sale to you. Was there anything about those individuals that encouraged you to proceed with the sale? What were they?

- What about the sales transactions you walked away from? Was there something about the person that discouraged you from moving forward? What was it?
- How can you replicate those positive interactions that you have experienced toward what you are selling now?
- What traits do you think people most often see in you?
- If there is one trait you could change starting today, what would it be?
- Think about a difficult time when something went wrong. How could you have been better prepared? If you could go back to that moment, what would you say to be more encouraging to yourself?

For without the hard work, you certainly cannot make a success of life.
—Theodore Roosevelt, *The River of Doubt: Theodore Roosevelt's Darkest Journey*

Your Takeaways

What are some takeaways, learning lessons, reflections that come to mind after reading this chapter? What stood out to you? Take a moment to write those thoughts out here:_______________________

____

____

____

____

____

____

____

____

CHAPTER 3

Looking at Failure Differently

I am not judged by the number of times I fail, but by the number of times I succeed, and the number of times I succeed is in direct proportion to the number of times I can fail and keep trying.
—Tom Hopkins, *How to Master the Art of Selling*[1]

In the 1980s a man by the name of Tom Hopkins published the book *How to Master the Art of Selling* based on his experiences in selling real estate. He went on to become a sales guru. Eventually he started an annual sales mastery bootcamp in Scottsdale, Arizona. During this three-day, grueling mental bootcamp, attendees had the opportunity to network and hear different motivational speakers on a variety of subjects. Topics included leadership, sales, and investment strategies. Participants would walk out of these sessions feeling as if they could conquer their own personal Mt. Everest.

The top headliner, of course, at the bootcamp was Tom Hopkins himself, who took participants through his videos and curriculum on mastering sales. Throughout the event, attendees heard from him often, and over the course of three days, they could earn points for passing quizzes, tests, and pop-up challenges. There were, at the time, approximately 650 points spread out among thirty-plus workbook pages of words to internalize. It was almost like trying to learn a new language within a forty-eight-hour time span. The carrots they dangled at the start of the event to absorb all the techniques and earning these points were several awards perched onstage. They glistened underneath the warmly focused glow of the ballroom lights. The trophies were in the shape of a phoenix rising from the ashes. The first-place winner received not only a phoenix trophy but also a prized piece of art. It is the kind of art that ends up in an attic to be discovered years later only to have amazingly increased in value. Above all, though, bragging rights among competitive peers in attendance was probably the biggest motivator for everyone.

I participated in the Tom Hopkins Sales Mastery Bootcamp twice. More than just bragging rights, I really wanted one of those shiny mythical bird trophies. The first time was in 2008. My wife even joined me and participated in the event. Despite my best efforts on the first go around, I exhibited a poor showing in obtaining points. After leaving for that first time, I knew that if I made it out to the event again, I could do better. The following year, a larger group of leaders from our company went back to Scottsdale, Arizona. I studied, memorized, and focused hard over those three days. Despite being at a nice resort, I ignored everything but memorizing what Tom told me. It was probably a good thing that my wife decided to let me go alone this time. I worked hard and paced around the Fairmont Scottsdale Princess focused on memorizing and practicing everything repeatedly. As nice as it was, I did not even think about enjoying any time at the pool.

By the end of the event after everything was tallied up, I had obtained 648 points out of 650 total available. Incredible! It is hard to put into words how much of a feat this was. It was only a couple of words I had missed out of all the testing and requirements. I felt like my efforts were amazing enough to win me a placement on the podium of glory next to Mr. Hopkins himself. That phoenix was in the bag and maybe even that art piece as well that could eventually collect dust in my attic.

The ballroom was filled with hungry, mentally beaten sales leaders. And the winners were announced one by one. Looking down at my point total I was smiling inside because I thought surely as the third-place winner was called I would be next or maybe even I would receive first place. It turned out I did not get any award or any recognition at all. Suffice to say that I was disappointed. We ended up going to the staff at the conclusion of the event and I showed them my scores, points, quizzes, and tests. I had only missed two points during the entire bootcamp; that was it. I think they were surprised that I had gotten so far and that I had even come up to question them. Tom Hopkins had disappeared at this point and so his team said they would investigate the situation and get back to me.

A month or so later out of the blue, we received a large box at our corporate office. Sure enough, a mythical bird trophy rose from the ashes of those Styrofoam popcorn pieces in that box. The Tom Hopkins Sales Mastery Bootcamp team relented and had decided to recognize me with third place. I still have my workbook from that event up on my shelf at home.

As the years have passed since then, most of what I shoved in my head from my time at that bootcamp has evaporated from my mind. This seems to happen because we as humans can only remember so much of what we read and hear. At least that's the way it is for me. I also have no idea at this point where the phoenix trophy ended up. The last time I remember seeing it, I believe it was in the back of a storeroom, covered with dust. Despite not retaining most of the material, there is one piece of the curriculum that has not ceased to stay with me. It is a section specifically talking about failure and how to face it when it comes our way. If you are alive, you'd better believe it will eventually come your way. Instead of viewing failure negatively, we have an opportunity to view it in a different light.

One of the ways Tom Hopkins launched his career was through his books and resources he wrote on the topic of sales. In *How to Master the Art of Selling*, as well as his bootcamp, Hopkins talks about how to respond to, and be prepared for, failure. To summarize the message simply in Hopkins's words: "I never see failure as failure."

One of the biggest inhibitors for growth and success is when we succumb to the *feeling* of failure. An *LA Times* article in 2015 cited a study by Linkagoal that surveyed over a thousand adults. The survey indicated that 31 percent of adults cited that they had a greater fear of failure than spiders or being home alone.[2] A 2018 Norwest Ventures Partners study indicated that 90 percent of CEOs "admit fear of failure keeps them up at night more than any other concern."[3] Did you know that an intense fear of failure has a medical term known as "Atychiphobia"? This word, just like character, is also derived from the Greek language. Specifically, it comes from the Greek word, *atyches*, which means, "unfortunate." People who suffer from atychiphobia avoid any potential circumstance that could lead to an unsuccessful outcome. It would be very unfortunate to consciously or subconsciously not take a step toward anything in which we see the potential to fail.

The fear of failing and self-doubt lead to some of the worst lies we can tell ourselves on the path of life. It is challenging to fight against these thoughts. Social pressures and outside influences will get you to start questioning yourself and say things like:

- I can't . . .
- I'll never . . .
- I'm not . . .
- This won't work out.
- What if they don't like me?
- What if I'm not good enough?
- Why bother?

- I don't have enough experience.
- I don't have anything to contribute . . .

Dwelling on statements such as these will rob you of potential success and opportunities that you might otherwise have. It will cause you to give up too soon when the next successful venture might be just past the next call you make. We need to train our minds to look at the way we see failure in a whole new way. Instead of seeing failures as dead ends, we can start seeing beyond them as opportunities for fresh beginnings.

Beginnings and opportunities for what?

- To learn:
  Learn from our mistakes.
  Learn new methods of delivery.
  Learn what works and what doesn't.
- To grow:
  Grow yourself.
  Grow the people who work with and around us.
- To practice skills.
- Build resiliency.
- Strengthening our character.
- Sharpen our wisdom.

Here are three quick stories on this.

What If They Turned out to Be Good?

One time our company had an opportunity to manage a nice asset in the Mid-Atlantic. A gentleman and his wife had been in the restaurant industry for many years. This would be the first hotel that they purchased and owned. A contact of ours found out that we would be doing a sales presentation and potentially working for this family. This contact called us specifically about this owner. They told my father and me that we should not do business with this person. They referenced a video and a couple of news articles about them that indicated this potential client could be a problem for us down the road.

One of our operations team members saw this material as well and said we should probably avoid proceeding any further. The thoughts of self-doubt and fear started creeping in for us. Should we proceed with taking a chance and continue trying to work with this person? The hotel itself was exactly what we were adept at operating. Besides the negative comments regarding the owners themselves, everything else seemed great. In the end, we did not listen to the outside influences. This owner ended up being one of our favorite ones to work with. We spent many years working with this family and made hundreds of thousands worth of fees. We did not ask, "What if the owner turned out to be bad?" and not continue forward. No, we asked, "What if they turn out to be good?"

And they did.

The Answer Is Always No Unless You Ask

Another time we had been managing a property in Virginia for a couple years. As time went by, this client started to not like the way the property was being run. They felt that the hotel would do better in the hands of another operator, so they provided us with a termination letter. In most cases, when a business relationship has ended, you move on and probably never speak to that person or group again. The self-doubt questions that come up are, "They will never work with us again," or, "We will not be able to earn their business back."

Again, be careful not to feed yourself definitive negative statements like this. I have always felt whenever possible we should call old clients and past leads that have dismissed our company or me. What is the worst that can happen anyway? The worst that can happen is they will not call you back or will provide zero response or will simply say, "No thanks." That's the way it is for every cold call or email you send. So, really, what are you afraid of?

After that owner fired us, I continued to stay in touch with her periodically. I checked in with genuine care and concern, asking how things were progressing. One day the owner expressed some frustrations they were having with the group that had been hired after us. I asked if they would be willing to give us another shot at managing the property again. They said they would give us another opportunity. Upon our reappointment this time around, we did well enough to help improve the value of the asset so they could eventually sell the property at top dollar. For a long time after that, this client kept looking for another hotel to buy so they could have us manage that one for them as well. If I had gone down the negative road, both they and our company would not have ultimately benefited.

You do not know unless you ask. If you feel you will fail by asking, then you are guaranteed to lose. You don't know unless you try. If you feel you will fail by trying, then again it will be for certain that you do not win. That would truly be *atyches* would it not? That client who hired our company back is one of two owners in my career thus far that returned after leaving. That is two more than zero. It is always worth keeping lines of communication open. Keep your bridges to relationships in good repair.

Beyond What If . . .

Cold calling, I believe, has become something of a lost art. Cold calling, or exploratory calls, are when you reach out to someone you would like to speak with, and they are not anticipating that call. They may have heard of your company, but they do not know who you are. Typically, in most cases you are met with forces of resistance in the form of secretaries (which happened a lot more years ago), office managers, or personal assistants. Now you typically must hunt through numbers or contacts in hopes of even leaving a message. Often you send wishful messages into the void of cyberspace and wait for a reply that may never come.

I remember calling a gentleman's office, and the lady on the phone asked me if so-and-so was expecting to hear from me. I said, "No, but they're going to like what they will hear." She patched me through to this individual, and we stayed in touch for a while, looking for prospective opportunities to work together on.

Before making the cold call, or sending the impromptu text, social media message or email, we come face-to-face with a feeling of potential failure. We take the question, "What if?" down the dark path versus taking the question in our mind down the light path of opportunity. Of course, they may say, "No, thanks." Yet what if they say, "Yes"?

This goes beyond just making sales calls. It revolves around many aspects of life. If you personally feel you should reach out to someone to ask for forgiveness, provide encouragement, express concern, let them know you care, let them know you love them, or anything like that, don't be afraid to do so. If these thoughts strike you in the moment, do not wait to carry them out. Better that you try and potentially fail than automatically miss out on making a positive impact on someone else. You want as many people as possible to warmly remember the day you crossed into their path, right?

Going back to sales specifically, I have come to embrace dialing a number and looking forward to whatever happens once a voice starts speaking on the other line. If you do not have a number, you can attempt something similar by sending an email or message on a social platform. You can train your mind to look forward in anticipation of the unknown and embracing uncertainty and welcoming failure.

George W. Dudley and Shannon L. Goodson conducted a study in the 1980s and wrote a book called *The Psychology of Selling.* In their study they determined that those in sales who struggled with call reluctance averaged $40,000 in commissions per year. However, those who had overcome this problem averaged over $200,000.[4] If we learn to welcome failure and overcome being gripped by fear of it, then we will simply go further. This could mean more profit as well.

On one occasion, I was making my way down from upstate New York for a flight the next morning out of Newark, New Jersey. While on the drive, I listened to a sermon that had been recorded at a prominent, well-known church. The guest speaker who spoke was a world-renowned photographer and artist named Jeremy Cowart. As Cowart started wrapping up his talk, he told everyone about a hotel concept that would center on giving back to people in need. Many aspects of the project/property would be equipped in ways to help others. For example, a portion of a guest's nightly stay would go toward helping an individual or charity. He called it the "Purpose Hotel." The tag line he had for it was, "Change the world in your sleep."[5]

As I listened, I thought immediately that our company would be able to help. I figured I would reach out and let him know I would be happy to help in any way I could. That evening when I got to my hotel room late, I looked up Cowart's website, compiled a message, and hit the send button. I had no idea if he would respond or not, but I was welcoming failure. It was Wayne Gretsky who famously said, "You miss 100 percent of the shots you don't take."[6]

I went to sleep, not sure what would become of it. The next day I received a call, and it was Cowart on the other end of the line! After talking for a little while, I ended up planning a trip to meet him in Franklin, Tennessee. Over the years we have continued to stay in touch. I hope that one day the Purpose Hotel will come to fruition, whether I am a part of it or not.

Had I not had a willingness to fail, I wouldn't have had the opportunity to connect with someone on an amazing project. Cowart was the other person in the story who took a risk by calling me back. He could have easily dismissed the message and kept on going. You and I also have opportunities to be the person on the other side of the equation who answers the call versus making it. Taking risks by being on the other side takes time to build discernment and wisdom. Eventually, though, you will have a better feeling for when you acknowledge fear but take a chance on responding anyway.

In Jack Canfield's book, *The Success Principles*, one of his points that I have tried to take with me is what Canfield calls, "feeling the fear and doing it anyway." He says, "Successful people understand that fear is something to be acknowledged, experienced, and taken along for the ride."[7] I would also add to Canfield's thoughts by saying, "Do what might simply be uncomfortable for you."

To be transparent, one of the things I dislike doing is speaking publicly. I am not as fearful as some people who would rather face death than stand in front of a crowd. It's just not something I like to do. Because of this, I have made it a point that whenever and wherever possible, I will do my best to speak. That could mean delivering a message, sharing a story on a presentation, participating on a panel, or having a conversation on a podcast. I recently had the opportunity to officiate a wedding. I had never done this before. But I've trained myself that if someone asks me if I would be willing to speak, I will probably raise my hand and say, "Yes."

Sometimes the uncomfortable direction is the one you should take because it forces you to stretch yourself. It is just like cardio exercise or lifting weights. Muscles pushed beyond the comfort zone, stretch, tear, and get stronger over time. Some of the best experiences, situations, sales calls, and learning lessons you will encounter will happen because you stretch yourself outside your parameters of comfort. Leadership expert John Maxwell says, "Get out of your comfort zone but not your gift zone."[8] You have the gifts and the abilities, and you can accomplish a lot in life. While embracing your gifts, seek to step beyond what you're comfortable with. Stretch yourself so you *have* to grow. The worst thing that can happen is you fail and are given the opportunity to learn, grow, and try again. The next time you do try, there will be more wisdom established as a stronger foundation beneath you.

Reflection on the Sales Mastery Bootcamp

What I gathered from that Tom Hopkins bootcamp is that I can, given the circumstances, be motivated enough to accomplish whatever I set my mind to. The same is true for you. Our brains are powerful. Walt Disney often said, "If you dream it, you can do it." If you believe it, you can achieve it.

The Right Number of Eggs in a Basket

After our Virginia owner sold the property, they had us start looking at different opportunities to purchase elsewhere. That was great. As time went along, though, we kept reviewing one potential acquisition after another without getting anywhere. This has happened many times over the years with different individuals and groups that have not hired us yet.

My point is that if you want to be effective in sales, be careful about putting all your eggs in one basket with either a current or prospective client. Be careful not to spend too much time chasing opportunities with one person or group. Putting all your eggs in one basket can put too much pressure on the successful outcome of that basket. Spread the love, know when to move on, and be there for them when the time is eventually right.

Listen To Your Mom or Someone You Trust

I shared a story about a property we managed in the Mid-Atlantic. Several people told us not to work for that ownership group. However, it was a great decision that we did not end up listening to those folks in that situation. Another time, many years later, we had an opportunity to manage a beautiful new property in Central Florida. This time my mom saw news articles and videos about this owner. She told us that she did not have a good feeling about us entering into an agreement with this group. The hotel was going to be beautiful. The location was amazing. Again, we were not considering what would happen if the owner turned out to be bad. We saw the videos and said to ourselves, "What if they turned out to be good?"

It turned out that the relationship with this owner turned out to be bad. The principal of the group became one of the angriest individuals I have ever had to interact with in my life. Some people get mad and frustrated for a variety of justifiable reasons in a moment or for a period. This person's spirit was soaked in anger, and it affected everyone it came across. The videos we saw prior to getting involved with this group were in fact very reflective of the experiences we had with them. When your mom or someone you trust provides discernment, it may be wise to listen!

Ideas

Raise Your Hand

When you are at a conference or seminar, after a speech or panel discussion concludes, there may be time for Q&A. Any time you have an opportunity to stand up at a mic or raise your hand to ask a question, you should do so. This will provide you with a captive audience to briefly share who you are and which company you are with. *Then* you ask your question. You never know who else may be in the room that will want to come and talk with you afterward because of the question you asked.

Change the Color of the Shirt

I once attended a business event that had an evening reception followed by dinner. I was talking to someone at my table who was with a vendor company we were not working with at the time that handled different kinds of promotional items. Always make sure to get to know the people you are sitting with at your table. We got to talk about his company and at some point, I asked how they were able to sell so many items. He eventually told me that sometimes they will take the same products they have and simply change the color. He said by periodically changing the color, it catches different people's eyes. It may make the same product look fresher. He also said it does not cost them that much to make changes like this. Maybe there is a product, experience, or an idea you are selling that does not seem to be catching on. It may be that interest in it has been waning over time. Perhaps now is the time to try changing the color of what you're selling. Adjust the look so that it catches people's eyes in a new way.

Questions to Consider

- Can you remember a time when you felt that you failed? Looking back now, do you view that experience differently?
- What is something you have thought about trying or dreamed about doing but have not started yet? What is holding you back?

Only those who dare to fail greatly can ever achieve greatly.
—Robert F. Kennedy

Your Takeaways

What are some takeaways, learning lessons, or reflections that come to mind after reading this chapter? What is something you can carry with you forward? Take a moment to write out those thoughts here:

____

____

____

____

____

____

____

____

CHAPTER 4

Preparedness

A person's gift opens doors for him and brings him before the great.
—Proverbs 18:16

When you receive a call or inquiry from a prospective client, typically they brief you on the summary of what they are working on and what they are looking for. During these early exploratory conversations, you determine whether you are, can, or should proceed to the next stage of the business relationship. There are several different stages and directions you can go.

- Based on your business, you may quickly realize in this initial conversation that it does not make sense to continue having discussions. It may not be the right fit, because the services they are looking for are something you cannot provide. Hopefully you part as friends and leave a bridge built between you.

- It may mean you pause for now and revisit connecting later.
- The conversation could create follow-up items so that further exploration can be done.
- Typically, the path will lead you to an eventual in-person onsite meeting. We have arrived at a time in history where a lot of interactions can and are done virtually. This works in many cases to a degree. However, nothing can fully replace an in-person visit where you can look someone in the eyes. There are also only so many things you can get a good handle on virtually. The best way to get a feel for something (particularly real estate) is to see the location or project in person. There is simply no way to fully capture the nuances of the surroundings unless you do this.
- My point with the above is: We should seek to get in front of someone physically and see their project physically, assuming initial conversations make sense. If you are trying to sell someone on a project or idea the inverse is true, try to get the person in front of you.

Thinking You're Prepared, but . . .

When I first started working in a business development position, our company had an opportunity to potentially look at a new ground-up project in Dana Point, California. We received a message one day from a guy whom I'll call Matthew Dantes. Based on my initial conversation with Dantes I felt the best thing to do would be to meet him in person. It was going to be a sizeable hotel project in a dream location. The only negative I knew right off the bat was that he was looking for us to potentially contribute equity to the deal. This is known as "having skin in the game." It means you are contributing money into the deal and will have some level of ownership in it as well. Doing this is a way for you or your company to show that there is commitment and belief in the project. It is also generally a way to guarantee your company having the opportunity to manage the project. Many groups such as ours do this, but our company at the time simply was not able to contribute equity or key money.

The opportunity was tempting, though. The projections seemed favorable. The initial renderings of the hotel were the kind of sweet carrot on a stick that make you want to do anything to get it signed up. However, I knew we would not be able to contribute any type of investment to this project. Regardless, I was determined to go out to California and give this prospective client the reasoning and logic why we would be a great company for them anyway. I would also explain why, for our company (or any group like us for that matter), contributing equity was not in their best interest. I felt prepared and confident to deliver this message in person.

At least I thought I did.

I coordinated a time to meet with Matthew Dantes in California at none other than the iconic Beverly Hills Hilton. Normally, you would connect in the lobby, but we planned to meet out by the pool. I do not know why we decided to do this. I think it was his idea. It was a swirl of sun, posh, awesomeness, and intimidation all mixed together in the carafe of Hollywood glamor. It felt like something out of a movie. I arrived at the property in my rental car and probably self-parked instead of using the valet. Nothing against valet, I just park my own car when I can. I made my way to the pool and waited in my suit next to half-dressed swimmers and sunbathers. Sweat was building on my forehead under the California sun. Thankfully, I did not have issues with this suit other than it was probably a little too big for me, and I was getting hot. Suddenly, cue the music, Dantes came strutting into the pool area with his designer shades, shirt unbuttoned, and chest hair exposed under a long gold chain.

We exchanged pleasantries, talked for a little, and then came the eventual moment of truth. Dantes asked, "Would you guys consider contributing equity into this deal?" To which I replied, "You know, Matthew, we don't believe it's actually in your best interest for us to do that." To which he replied, "Why?"

As soon as the question left his mouth, my mind totally drew a blank. I had thought I was prepared. In the back recesses of my mind, I knew the three key bullet points I'd prepared to answer his question confidently. However, nothing was able to come out of my mouth. I was literally only able to utter, "umm" and "ahh." Just noise, stuttering, and stammering came out of me! Dantes finally broke the awkward silence and steered the conversation in a different direction. Before veering off, though, he threw in something like, "Get back to me on that," and a look that said, "This guy is a waste of my time."

What happened to me?

In the heat of this moment at the swanky pool with Mr. Dantes, I blanked in my moment of truth. I was unprepared to communicate what needed to be said. Even though I knew it was something that would most likely come up in the conversation.

I ended up leaving the Beverly Hills Hilton to go see the location that Dantes and I had discussed. He told me I would be connecting with his associate in Dana Point, but I did not see anyone there. In the end this deal did not go anywhere. Time passed and Matthew Dantes truly did want investors and money to do the project. However, to my knowledge I do not believe it happened. It is okay that this project did not come together for us. Some of the best opportunities and outcomes will be when a deal that does not make sense does not come to fruition. The last thing you want is to be in a lose–lose situation with someone or some project.

What stuck in my head though from this experience was the importance of preparation. I was not as prepared as I thought I was to be able to respond to a question I absolutely knew was coming.

Being prepared is essential if you are going to be successful with sales and other aspects of life. If you want to get ahead, you must prepare yourself physically and mentally. When it comes to physical preparation, we typically have an idea of what it takes. Proper sleep, nutrition and exercise are all important. Mental preparation may be a little harder for some to get their head around. Pun intended.

Mental prep may include a number of possibilities.

Look at yourself in the mirror and speak affirming statements.

Over the years I have had the opportunity to work with my father in and out of many different sales meetings. As I mentioned previously, before going into these meetings, we would find a bathroom in the office building. Not necessarily to use it but rather to look at ourselves in the mirror. He would get himself all hyped up and start repeating phrases such as, "I like myself" and "I'm a great salesman!" These are affirming statements, and the "great" part always came out sounding as if it should be in a cereal commercial with a big orange cartoon tiger. Why did we do this? Part of preparedness finds its footings and stability in confidence. I can know my product and know what I plan to say, but unless I am mentally prepared and confident in myself, the results can end up sounding unconvincing and unbelievable. Not the kind of "unbelievable" reaction we want either.

We would walk into those meetings, anticipating the prospective client would be happy and delighted to connect with us. Our body language and countenance would be smiling and upbeat. Did it always work? No, not always. However, often prospective clients would pick up on these verbal and non-verbal clues and respond positively. If nothing else, starting off this way helps leave a great lasting first impression. Next time you go into a meeting with a prospective client or situation, speak affirming statements to yourself. Get mentally hyped. This can be done daily as well if there are objectives you are seeking to accomplish. Objectives could be anything from losing weight, learning a skill, training for a marathon, or spending less time on social media. Put notes and affirming statements in front of you so that you can strengthen yourself mentally.

Review as much knowledge that you have available about a prospective client and the project/opportunity they are discussing with you.

This is done through studying material given to you or researching information that must be dug through on your own. Digging through research may involve using different tools and platforms. It will probably mean you have to visit and experience the competition or market to fully get a handle on where the areas of opportunity are.

I did a study for a project in Manhattan once. I was hesitant to stay at the subject property we were reviewing because it was at the bottom of the barrel as far as hotel rank in the city. I knew it was not going to be great. However, I could see my grandfather in my mind asking, "How are you going to know unless you go and stay there?" I booked the room and was glad I ended up staying to experience the property firsthand. I was able to pick up on a lot of areas for improvement like making the lobby less dark and foreboding at night. When it comes to real estate and hospitality, you can only do so much from a distance. Sometimes there is no way of getting your mind around something unless you fully immerse yourself in it. Doing so helps you pick up on nuances you would not otherwise see. From there you can speak more confidently about the challenges and changes to be implemented. Why? Because you have experienced it firsthand for yourself.

For several years I worked at Walt Disney World Resort in Central Florida. Every position I worked in during my time with Disney we had to experience multiple positions, taste the foods, see where everything was located, watch the show, and so on. I worked for a little while at Disney's Polynesian Resort at their main restaurant called Ohana. I can still smell that pineapple bread that every guest received upon arrival. I hope they still do this. In addition to saying, "Aloha" and "Mahalo" a lot, I spent time on the dessert line, served tables, sang happy birthday to celebrities, and observed positions that I was not going to be in on a regular basis. Why? It helped me understand the roles of the other team members I would be working with. It also helped me build confidence with my understanding of the way the restaurant worked.

Knowledge and understanding builds confidence. You certainly feel more prepared—except for that one time I slung shrimp off a skewer in a lady's lap. I think my superiors were thankful I was hosting and not serving tables.

Think through your thoughts and ideas you want to share.

This includes bouncing them off people you trust in your life for their feedback and perspective. It is helpful to get thoughts from those who are outside looking in and are not close to what you are working on. We should welcome criticism and advice that will help make us better. Be careful not to overthink things.

Practice your presentation and what you're going to say in advance, so you feel more comfortable speaking through your talking points.

This can be done in the car, in front of a mirror, in front of friends, or wherever you feel most comfortable. Speaking it out loud helps you get more comfortable and fluid with the words you are going to say.

Rehearse responses to known roadblocks that will most likely come up in conversion.

Before going into that situation at the Beverly Hills Hilton, I should have practiced my responses more thoroughly in advance. Over time you will hear familiar concerns and questions that potential prospects and clients bring up. With experience you will get better with your responses and the way that you communicate them.

Have your material together, ready to go in advance of any meeting or presentation.

Do not wait until the last minute if it can be avoided. This includes allowing adequate time to be prompt or early before a meeting starts. If you are sharing information, it means arriving early to set up everything in advance. I tried to do this in West Virginia, but I ended up splitting my pants and getting rained on. But normally things go better than that.

Preparedness also takes shape in other ways. An example of this is preparing your calendar, hours, and days with good time management. By doing the above, you will be more apt to sell effectively regardless of the environment you find yourself in. That environment could be a pre-planned meeting by a pool in Hollywood, at a table during a tradeshow, or an impromptu conversation in an elevator.

Your effectiveness with preparation will translate into how well you do at execution. Execution of preparedness helps retain long-lasting business, friendships, connections, and relationships. It builds confidence and greater security into what you are trying to sell.

Another opportunity I had at Walt Disney World Resort was being a part of the opening team for Expedition Everest. This is a high-speed roller coaster at Disney's Animal Kingdom Theme Park. Despite causing some guests to throw up by the time they got off, it was a very popular ride. We had guests get on that attraction so many times there were a couple guys who even got tattoos of a yeti on their body. One person we even called the yeti man. I'm thankful for this experience because we got a chance to participate with all the preparation and effort that went into turning an idea into a reality. Disney is well known for how much preparation and thoroughness they take before finalizing or executing a project. It took Disney Imagineers six or more years to get Pirates of the Caribbean in Shanghai Disney open and operating. In the case of Expedition Everest, Imagineers spent a good amount of time in Nepal researching and gathering information. They did not just gather facts, they captured pictures, smells, and more to help transport guests to a whole new world. Hmm, that kind of sounds familiar, doesn't it?

All this preparation helps create a story of authenticity that guests can see and feel while experiencing the attraction. They work from the minor details outward to help accomplish this from a distance. It is carried through the queue (the line people wait in), all through the ride, and through the gift shop on the way out. Preparation goes beyond just the theming. While opening the ride, there are many tests, and a lot of training is conducted in advance so that all cast members are ready for the day when guests arrive. The work and effort up front help you and the team be as ready as you can be. Of course, as time progresses and new situations occur, learning and adjustments often need to be made. Was I nervous? Of course I was. But I never felt unprepared with any position I worked in from the start.

Just because you may effectively prepare does not mean you will not need to adjust. Prepare as much as you can in advance but be willing to adapt. Successful salespeople know that they may need to tweak and adjust their presentation. They may—and most likely will—need to go back to their team and discuss areas for improvement based on feedback and responses being given. If you do not feel prepared for a given position, continue to ask questions of those you work with. Be honest and up front if there are parts and pieces you do not understand.

It's all about setting yourself up for success. The importance of preparedness cannot be underscored enough in how it translates to being effective at selling. There are a couple of different avenues when it comes to this, as I have already alluded to. The first avenue deals with mental preparation. This is how we train our mind prior to entering any sales situation. The second avenue deals with a combination of mental/physical preparation. This is the route where we gather intel about a product, service, prospect, dream, or idea. It is getting our arms around the details. The more we can gather and know about our product, the better we are able to intelligently speak to it.

Know the background to your product or service.

If you do an internet search for "greatest salespeople of all time," you will come across several recognizable names. A name that you may not recognize is a woman who worked for Steinway & Sons for many years in New York City: Erica Feidner. During her employment with the company, she sold over $40 million worth of instruments, namely pianos. How did she make that happen and become so effective at selling a product that can cost musicians many thousands of dollars?

Growing up, Feidner lived in a house that had twenty-six pianos and seven pianists. Their home welcomed family and friends from all around the world to stay and play music together. Her plan was to become a professional musician. However, an injury to her hand altered the course of her life. Through various sets of circumstances, Feidner ended up working at Steinway & Sons. Even though she became lauded as a top salesperson, Feidner would say that she typically saw the word "sale" as a "four letter word." Feidner viewed then, as she does now, that she is more of a "piano matchmaker" than anything else. Having been around pianos and players most of her life, she became very apt at reading body language, tone of voice, eye contact, and speaking in a language that the customer would understand. For example, if the customer had an engineering background, Erica could point out features that would be of most interest to them. In other words, she could customize the experience and, in her words, "pair the personality of the piano to the person."[1]

Erica was prepared with the knowledge of the products she was selling. She was also prepared with the knowledge and experience of how to play music. Because of this she was better prepared to match specific products with customers as she got to know more about them individually. You may not be selling pianos, but you are selling something. What areas of your business do you feel you need to have a better understanding of? How about yourself personally? How are you doing at developing and selling your character to others?

When we get better at mental and physical preparation, we give ourselves more opportunities to win. We are also more apt to see areas that can strengthen our character. Seeing those areas, we can strengthen now is great preparation for our future selves.

Ideas

Bring the Lion.

There is a story about how Disney's Animal Kingdom Park came about. Apparently, Disney executives were skeptical about the idea of a new theme park. They were not so convinced that guests would be interested in another zoo or park around animals. The now-legendary Disney Imagineer Joe Rhode had the idea of bringing a real-life lion into the boardroom. Seeing an actual lion was very compelling. Ultimately, the park ended up coming to life and guests have loved it ever since.

Think about a visual you can bring to your next board meeting or conversation. Sometimes stories and visuals are more powerful than stats on a paper or computer screen. What can you visually share or emotionally convey that will help create a deeper connection with those you are presenting to?

Bring the lion.

Share Experiences.

Help steer others toward a clearer vision based on your experiences. I often tell people that I have been in the hospitality industry for over twenty years. Over the course of that time, I have seen a lot of variable situations happen. I can confidentially tell others what will work and what will not. Part of what others will buy into is your expertise and time within a given field. They will be able to feel it from your answers and the knowledge you are able to convey. If you are just starting out, then find others who are further along than you. Ask them about their experiences. Ask them, if they were you at your age or current position, what would they suggest doing next?

Keep Your Notes with You.

If you are going to a presentation or meeting, keep your key points with you in the notes section of your phone. In the event something slips your mind, you will be able to refer to it.

Questions to Consider

- Can you think of time when you felt like you were not prepared? What did you learn from that experience?
- Is there an area of the of your current job or position where you feel insecure or nervous? What can you do to get more comfortable with this area?
- What are some best practices or ideas you have experienced from individuals or companies that you would like to replicate into what you are selling?

Preparedness is the ultimate confidence builder.
—Vince Lombardi

Your Takeaways

Did something hit you while you were reading this chapter? It may be an area you need to take time to prepare more in. What is your takeaway? Take a moment to write those thoughts out here: ______

____
____
____
____
____
____
____
____
____
____
____
____

CHAPTER 5

Confidence and Building Effectiveness

Belief, I decided. Belief is irresistible.
–Phil Knight, *Shoe Dog: A Memoir by the Creator of Nike*

Heading down Granada Boulevard through a small town called Ormond Beach, Florida, you will eventually connect with Beach Street. Heading south down this road takes drivers along the intercoastal waterway in Volusia County, with sparkling water, moss-covered trees, and homes that have seen their fair share of storms. If you blink, it is easy to miss a little sign on your left that says "Ames House." The casual passerby or vacationer would not have any idea that this location was formerly the summer home for the last living Union general of the American Civil War, Adelbert Ames.

Ames, who lived to the age of ninety-seven, is an often-overlooked character in the story of the war and history of the United States. Originally from Maine, Ames graduated second in his class at West Point. With his strong leadership he quickly rose through the ranks and became a general at thirty-four. Toward the end of the war, one of the last great bastions for the Confederacy was Fort Fisher in South Carolina. It was a nightmarish sandcastle designed to inflict maximum damage upon all soldiers who attempted an attack, whether by land or sea. The location, however, was important as the Union sought to take full control of the region and push on toward cutting off further access routes for the Confederates in Wilmington, North Carolina.

Having already battled once to take down the fort, the Union organized a concerted second attempt on January 15, 1865. Fort Fisher, along with its occupants, did not disappoint in their ability to take a toll on life. However, Union efforts succeeded due to an unintended diversion in the battle. As the fighting wore on, Ames entered at the head of the 2nd Brigade and stood firm in the middle of the action. Captain Lockwood, who took note of the unfolding situation, wrote that "Ames stood within this circuit of fire amid the fragments of his division; every brigade and almost all of the regimental commanders had fallen."[1] Incredibly, even though 659 members of his unit were either dead, wounded or missing, Ames went through battle unscathed."

Years prior to Fort Fisher, during the battle of Fredericksburg, Ames reflected on his leadership and the regiment he supported in 1862. He remembers being the only one who led his regiment into the fight out in front. Of that battle he stated, "My men now have confidence in me, and the battle taught them the necessity of discipline."[2] After seeing this bravery and confidence in action, Ames's men had no doubts about their leader. The seeds of character Ames sowed in his past blossomed during a pivotal moment at the Second Battle of Fort Fischer. In the heat of the battle on the sands of South Carolina, Adelbert Ames led by example and instilled confidence in his men.

Arriving at this point did not happen overnight. The confidence that Ames displayed was built up over time.

So, what are you and I building now within us that has an opportunity to be strengthened? What actions can you and I take now in the present that will translate positively for us in the future?

Over the years, Adelbert Ames garnered confidence not only in his men but consistently with his superiors as well. His units willingly followed him into battle. Commanding officers came to trust in his involvement during the engagements they faced. He gave his superiors confidence in his ability to effectively manage situations. Historian Harry King Benson states that "wherever circumstances placed him, he earned the encomiums of [his] superiors."[3] After the war, Ulyssess S. Grant would say, "If I had given him [Butler] two corps commanders like Ames, he would have made a fine campaign on the James and help[ed] materially in my plans."[4]

Grant was speaking of Major General Benjamin Franklin Butler, who led the 40,000-man army of the James. Butler's leadership and oversight was highly criticized as they lost many soldiers fighting the rebels along the James River in May 1864. Looking back, Grant would have been more confident in the outcome in battles that had ensued had a trusted leader such as Ames been more connected to those in command.

Would it not be amazing if we could give the people whom we work with and for that kind of strong confidence in us? How about those who are in our closest inner circle? Do they have the kind of confidence where they would look back and think to themselves, "I'm really glad I put them in the game, in charge of that project, or bought into what they were selling. I can really count on them."

Confidence for Your Battles

As we go through life, we will probably not face attackers with bayonets in a splintering fort on a sandy beach. We will, however, most certainly come up against other battles. In the world of sales and building character, battles are unavoidable. How well we react and respond to the ones we face, I believe, will translate into the output of success we achieve. We can set ourselves up for responding well through confident solid leadership. Whether spoken or not, confidence and leadership are absolutely desired by others. People are drawn to it, and not only are we drawn to great leadership, but we also need it within ourselves. Beyond being confident in selling, we should seek to be confident leaders ourselves.

One thing for sure is that when you face the battle of sales and selling in life, your confidence will be ambushed. The attacks will appear in all forms. They could come in the form of what feels like insurmountable odds, continual failure, and rejection. Attacks can show up in the form of discouraging words from others. People or companies directly or indirectly say, "You'll never make it," and, "You're not good enough." It could be within the unspoken pressures of your department to achieve, perform, and meet specific quotas. Yet your greatest battle will probably be the one in your own mind. You will fight against the negative words you repeatedly say to yourself.

Internalizing and thinking negative thoughts are something we all do. It's only a matter of time before confidence attackers appear in the repetitive lies we tell ourselves. Do not believe it when you say you are not good enough. You are. Do not believe it when you say you do not have the means or resources to make it happen. You either have them already or you can get them. We can all learn and grow every day.

Other people's confidence in you

What Ames displayed for himself, and his troops was confidence in the face of the seemingly impossible. They were going up against what had been an impenetrable fortress. Yet his troops believed in his example and resolved that they themselves could be successful.

Besides being a salesperson, I believe you are also a leader. The team members you lead, whether sales or otherwise, are looking for someone to lead them confidently and boldly. The conveyance of this creates an atmosphere that encourages creativity, optimism, fearlessness, desire to achieve, and aspirations for advancement. More people will want to work with you if they feel they can get further because of it. Whatever bus you are driving, they are going to want to get on. If you are driving the bus, then you need to make sure everyone who gets on finds the right seats. Perhaps as you go down the road, there may even be some that need to get off the bus.

I want to note that confidence should not equal arrogance. We as salespeople and leaders should know what we are talking about. There must certainly be a fundamental foundation of knowledge. Yet we need to be careful to know when to listen and not act as if we know everything. Great salespeople are good listeners. They may be knowledgeable, experienced in their field but do not act like know-it-alls. They are humble enough to not only be good listeners but also lifelong learners. There are several proverbs that reference watching the words you say. This takes good listening skills, patience, and discernment. An example is Proverbs 17:27 which says, "The one who has knowledge restrains his words, and one who keeps a cool head is a person of understanding."

Second, the prospective clients you are hoping to obtain will subconsciously and consciously notice a marked difference in how confident you are with the product you are selling. I have had people tell me that I am good at what I do. I then asked myself: Why would they say this? Part of the reason, I believe, has to do with the fact that I have been working in the field of hospitality for a while. I can confidently speak from experience because layers of applicable time in this field have built up beneath me. If you have not been in your role or industry for a while, that's okay. Understanding your product, service, dream, or idea, and being able to speak to it boldly, will help overcome lack of experience to a degree.

Regardless, if you are sheepish, unsure, or wavering in your delivery, people can sense it. I once had the opportunity to sell our company to an ownership group that had almost a dozen hotels. The portfolio had a mix of hotels in varying degrees of condition and quality. In discussing the portfolio internally with our team, there were a few properties in the portfolio that the company did not want to operate. One of the reasons was that the product types were more on the economy side of the scale. The team did not feel we would be as successful at operating them.

I understood not wanting to waste either party's time or money. I understood the reasoning and that as a company you want to do what makes the most sense for the business overall. You want there to be a win-win between you and the client. However, because I entered the sales scenario by saying we would manage most but not all, I did not feel confident about the sales relationship from the beginning. Even though from a macro perspective it was a great opportunity, our team had their doubts. Those doubts transferred to me, and my mental footing became unsteady as a result. Ultimately, another group was selected that was willing to manage all the hotels without any reservations. And they did it with a different pricing structure than we offered.

Despite not being selected, chosen, or hired, you must keep moving.

This situation, even though we did not end up getting the deal, was still a learning opportunity. Learning opportunities from losing are only negative if you see them that way. Viewed differently, they can be another notch in the belt of experience. Experience helps us build confidence. In sales and life, when we as people come against hardships and trials, we tend to retreat and hope to never get burned again. Yet jumping through hoops of fire and wading through adversity help sharpen our responses to people and circumstances. We are better able to address questions, encourage others, and savor true wins. As time progresses, we grow and build confidence in ourselves that we feel internally and others see externally.

After a period of about a year, the company that was hired instead of us in that situation ended up performing badly. We made a second attempt to work with this group. This time we collectively approached the opportunity with a different perspective and a willingness to be flexible. However, we still missed the boat and did not end up getting the opportunity to work together again a second time. The outcome may have been positive for us had we started off differently from the beginning.

Confidence we see in ourselves

We should seek to put ourselves out there. In high school I was invited to be a part of a rock band. A guy I knew must have seen me acting in one of the school musicals and felt that I could also do rock 'n' roll as well. They asked me to be the lead singer. I could not play an actual instrument, but I did have vocal cords, and I could put together lyrics for the songs. Our band's name was Blue Star. We put together a bunch of original songs, and we practiced in the basement of our drummer's house. We practiced a lot. Then we spent time and money in a recording studio and practiced some more.

One day we finally had the opportunity to play an actual show live in front of people. It was a battle of the bands at the college I was attending in western Maryland. We were the first band to perform, and we were also the band that came in last place. I don't think we lost because of a lack of practice. While it could be that the judges did not like the music, I think we lost because of a lack of playing in front of other people. If all we do is practice and never actually perform, then we will not fully grow. Nor will our confidence get stronger. That time at the battle of the bands was the one and only show we ever played. I still have the CD we recorded. The only problem is I do not have a CD player anymore.

If all we do is practice, we will struggle to gain confidence. And unless we seek to stretch ourselves, we will struggle to gain confidence.

Growing up I thought I would be a theater major. As a young kid through the first part of college, I was in a bunch of shows and musicals. That's probably how I ended up being the lead singer in a band. Believe it or not, I played the role of Danny in the musical *Grease*. As often as I have been on stage, I still do not really care for public speaking in person or virtually. Yet I push myself to participate in activities like this because I know it stretches me. The more I do something does not mean that I will necessarily like it more, it does, however, build confidence to be able to go into situations, knowing I can persevere. The same can be true for you. You and I can go into the same situations, and while we may not like them, we know we can get through them. We can be stronger by facing that which stretches us beyond our comfort zone.

Our objective should not be to seek recognition or trophies for practicing or losing. Rather, we should acknowledge that loss is a reward in and of itself. Through losing we can learn to be better losers *and* winners. We can learn to build confidence in ourselves for the storms and trials ahead. Doing this does not make circumstances any easier. But it will mentally prepare and give us confidence that we will be able to get past anything that comes our way.

Before I became CEO of our company, I was at a hotel conference and was going back to my room after a full day. I stopped and talked with someone who was also attending the conference. He asked what my position was with my company. I said, "Well, I guess I'm CEO." The guy said back to me, "You guess? You either are or you aren't." That was the last time I hesitantly replied regarding the leadership position I was in. I am not big on titles. I would often say while being in this role that I was the Chief Encouragement Officer of the company. Regardless, I either am, or I am not. Either you are or you are not.

People can tell when you are unsure of yourself. Be confident and proud of who you are and the leadership position you are fortunate to be in. Again, confidence does not translate to arrogance.

Confidence you give to others

One of the ways we give confidence to others is by exhibiting transparent belief in the product we're selling. Phil Knight, the founder of Nike, sold all sorts of products in his younger years. One day he had the opportunity to start selling shoes, and his sales took off. He reflected on why he was so much more successful at selling shoes than encyclopedias or mutual funds. He asked, "Why was selling shoes so different? Because I realized it wasn't selling. I believed in running. I believed that if people got out and ran a few miles every day, the world would be a better place, and I believed these shoes were better to run in. People sensing my belief, wanted some of that belief for themselves."[5]

Do you believe in what you are selling? Do you believe in yourself?

Another way we give confidence to others is through the demonstration of integrity. Who we are on Monday should be the same as who we are Sunday. Our life should not be varied depending on which piece is picked up and looked at. People should look at us, and what they see is what they should get. As someone of integrity, we can become human beings that people can rely on and trust. Clients and people know that we are looking for their best interests, that we follow through, and we are reliable. When people sense that about us, we bestow on them a layer of confidence. They will feel less likely to fail because they know there is someone they can count on—you.

Don't Give up on Yourself

The band I was a part of in high school had two drummers at different times. Unfortunately, our first drummer passed away at a young age. One day I got a call and was told that our friend had committed suicide. To my knowledge, he killed himself over a girl who had dumped him. I was shocked. His family was devastated, and I do not think they were ever the same. Our friend had lost confidence in himself to an extreme degree. This unfortunately happens all the time. People lose confidence in others, themselves, and their future. They lose hope and do not see a path forward.

If you have had those thoughts, or you are thinking through them now, my encouragement is to not give up on yourself. You can succeed.

You can persevere. You can win. It is never too late. There are people who love you and care for you. There are resources available to help. The first step forward is doing the most courageous action we can take, and that is to admit that we need help.

When both of our boys turned thirteen, we organized a coming-of-age two-mile walk around a lake near our home. We filled up a backpack with bricks and made them start waking. Stationed along the way were friends and family members who took a brick out of the backpacks. My wife and I took out the last bricks. The purpose of this walk was to teach our boys that they do not have to go through life alone. They have people who care about them and will help carry the weight.

The same is true for you. You do not have to go forward alone.

Keep moving forward.

Selling Internally

If you are working for an organization big or small, you will most likely have to get on the same page with the different departments in the company you work for. You will have to help sell them on a project that potentially everyone will be working on. The most grief you will probably get is from the operations team. They will typically be the ones to ask questions like, "Why are we doing this?" or, "Do we really want to do business with this group/person?" If you are seeking to do something great, get ready to face opposition in the form of doubt, resistance, and negativity.

Most people have a hard time believing in what is being sold until they can see results physically start to materialize. It is up to you as the salesperson to sell the story, the big picture, and the potential—in advance—to those you will be working with. Do as much due diligence as you can, be clear, welcome questions, listen, set expectations, paint a picture of positives, and give confidence.

Take a Leap

Throughout my grandfather's time at the helm of our family business, he and his partner took many risks. They built and developed many properties and projects around the Washington Metro area. He would say that there were many times he was not 100 percent confident the project would be totally successful. So, he would get himself as close to being as confident as possible. Then at some point he relied on faith for the remaining percentage. Eventually he would take that leap of faith.

In Chapter 3 I talked about looking at failure differently. One of the questions I asked at the end of the chapter was if there was something you have been thinking about trying or dreaming about doing? Perhaps you are not 100 percent confident it will be successful. What percentage would you give it? If you're almost there it may be time to rely on what you have put into it thus far. Make up the difference with faith in yourself and faith that God has your back no matter what.

Ideas

Seek to Actually Help People

Seek to help people with their investments. Those who are straightforward and honest with what makes sense and what does not are the ones I would like to work with. Wouldn't you agree? In the long run you and your company will ultimately achieve more in the end.

A Way to Read

There is a saying that "leaders are readers." It's sometimes said that most people have big TVs; successful people have big libraries. Even if you don't read a lot, read so that you can highlight things that stand out to you. One of the ways I like to read as I go through a book is to underline ideas, quotes, and statements that stand out to me. I then write the page number at the front of the book. This way I can easily go back to it without having to flip through trying to figure out where it was. Figure out ways of reading that work for you so you can reference what stands out to you. The benefits will be returned every time you review a book.

Questions to Consider

It is important to take time to understand, to the best of your abilities, your opposition (competition), and product. Whether you are new or have been around for a while, it is helpful to revisit questions on a periodic basis:

- What are the processes, procedures, and people needed to make my product work?
- Who are the experts internally and externally that I can reach out to?
- What are the benefits of what you are selling?
- What are the weaknesses?
- What are some of the success stories?
- What am I unsure about or afraid of?
- What is new and exciting about what I'm offering?
- What can you start investing in now that will pay off in the future?
- What is something you are working on that that you feel will require a leap or step of faith?
- Why have you not taken that step yet?

I think we should act by the best light we have or can command;
and even should we sometimes make mistakes,
we should not permit them to make us unhappy.
—Adelbert Ames[6]

Your Takeaways

Was there something that caught your attention when you were reading this chapter? It may be an area where you are lacking confidence and need to strengthen. What is your takeaway? Take a moment to write a thought or two out here:

CHAPTER 6

Perseverance

Do not both adversity and good
come from the mouth of the Most High?
—Lamentations 3:38

On July 2, 1968, at around 5 a.m., Neil Coakley was writing out his thoughts on the circumstances his company presently found themselves in. The business, as it was known at the time, was Coakley & Williams, Inc., a general contracting company that started seven years earlier in 1961. Neil and Fred Williams, my grandfather, had built and developed numerous properties around Washington, DC. Economic conditions under the Johnston administration had created a scarcity of money that translated to high interest rates and larger fees to be paid to lenders. Coakley hit letters on his typewriter in the early morning hours that day, explaining the various pickles they found themselves in.

The company owed almost two hundred thousand dollars. They had lost over six hundred thousand so far in foreclosures. Banks would not lend them money, subcontractors were threatening to sue, and creditors were closing in on them with personal guarantees that had been signed. Coakley noted, "We must never forget these times when all are against us. We could be wiped out at any time and not a soul would give a damn." He continues a few lines later, "When this storm subsides, and we are back to normal; we must always remember that if we survived, it was in spite of everyone else. It seems as though everyone is trying his or her best to cause our downfall. So, if we succeed, we will not owe anything to anyone as we will have survived through our own efforts."[1]

Do you ever have moments where you feel that everyone and everything is against you? Coakley's reflections in the heat of a difficult season speak to the varying degrees of what we will all face as we live life on earth. We will all face adversity and challenge. It's not a matter of if but of when. Sometimes it's caused by situations we create for ourselves out of failure, mistakes, or choices we make. Failure and mistakes are something we should embrace, learn, and grow from.

Other times, it's caused by forces and circumstances outside our control. How we respond when facing all forms of resistance is very telling in how the rest of our story has the potential to play out. We need to determine in our mind whether we will have a willingness to persevere or not. Goodness can grow and flourish out of all forms and reiterations of challenge.

I often say that great things do not come easily or without effort. When I was starting out in our company, I attended a large motivational event that was being held in downtown DC at what is now known as the Capitol One Arena. The place was packed. All kinds of headliners were there from sales legend Zig Ziglar to Colin Powell.

I do not remember any of it except for one of the breaks in between the top speakers. A group got up on stage, talking about a product they had created along with an in-person training program that went along with the purchase. Basically, the product or software helped people with their stocks and investments. Their pitch was something to the effect of, "Ladies and gentlemen, you need to watch the arrows on these investments. When they turn green, you buy, and when they turn red, you sell." It seemed so simple and easy! Why would I not want this?

Toward the end of their sales pitch, they said that anyone who signed up that day would receive a special price on the whole package. You would not believe the mad dash that people made to get to one of their tables. I made my way down to sign myself up. All I had to do was buy when it was green and sell when it was red. I just needed to get this product. Then: *Wait a minute, do I really need this?* I stopped in my tracks and thought to myself, *This is way too easy.* I went right back to my seat. I have never known anyone who made it rich off the product those people sold that day. And I never heard of that product or their seminar again.

Great things do not come without effort. Varying degrees of perseverance will be required of you.

The ability to persevere in the face of trials is a common thread in the living texture of those we perceive to be successful. Success can be viewed in several ways, and it means something different depending on who you ask. You could have been successful surviving in the woods alone for an extended period. You took one step at a time, persevered, and did not give up. You could be successful because you created a multimillion-dollar business through your perseverance through long hours, big risks, hiring great people around you, and demonstrating continual dedication. You could be successful because you feel you have arrived at a place of peace and contentment with the circumstances around you. You could be successful from escaping a sun-drenched pool in Hollywood and remembering what to say to a guy with gold chains around his neck. Different people define success differently.

In the case of sales, success can come in small or large achievements. This could be from connecting with a new lead at tradeshow or hitting your quota for the year. No matter what, if we are going to be successful at selling a product, service, a dream, idea, ourselves, or our character to others, we must build within us a resolve to persevere.

In the summer of 2015, I received an inquiry from a gentleman who owned a banquet and events facility in the mid-Atlantic. The facility itself is beautiful and right on the water. Back when I started talking to the owner, it was pretty much brand new. Conversations started off well. I sent a proposal for management and had him visit one of our full-service hotels. Time passed and I kept following up and following up. I had team members visit the banquet facility and provide their thoughts and feedback. We kept reviewing the terms of the agreement. Soon a whole year passed. Then things dropped off, but I kept following up periodically. Conversions bubbled up every once in a while.

One day years later I was driving in central Pennsylvania to look at another project. I got a call from the owner of this banquet and events facility. He asked me if it would be possible to connect in person. Coincidentally, I had some extra time during this trip, and the location was on my way back toward the airport I would be flying out of. When we met, I asked if now after all this time he really wanted to look at management of his facility. He said yes, and we got the agreement signed in November of 2021. That's almost six years since I first started our conversations together!

In another case back in 2016, I got connected to a group in the Southeast that was looking to do a mixed-use development in North Georgia. I will never forget the evening I flew into Atlanta with my brother-in-law, who had just started working in business development for us at the time. We rode around the market, reviewing and discussing all the eventual dreams and plans. Months and years went by, and this project never seemed to get underway. We talked to brands, ran projections repeatedly, and just when things might have started really moving, the pandemic hit. In addition to this project, we had others and had reviewed still more all over the state with nothing coming to fruition. That is, until December 2024, when our first opportunity finally came together with a signed agreement to manage a hotel they were purchasing. It would be another nine months before we were able to start managing the property. That is almost nine years of persistence before finally starting to work on a great project together.

In both cases I could have said long before the first year had passed that these opportunities were not worth my time. As you progress forward along your path of sales, you will gain a greater aptitude for discernment. You will eventually gain a better feeling for which deals (and the people behind them) are not worth following anymore. Over time you will get a sense of which ones are worth poking and checking in on every now and again. In the case of the Mid-Atlantic opportunity, I continued to persevere because I truly felt like one day an opportunity would come to fruition. One day the owner would change their mind and be ready to sign the agreement. That is what happened. I have had opportunities come together where the prospective client has literally said, "I feel like we need to work together because you have stayed in touch with me for so long."

Remember: If it's worth pursuing, persist. And persistence always pays. Sometimes that payment goes beyond monetary gain. Persistence pays with learning lessons, experience, growth, confidence, and building trust. This is applicable whether you are seeking to get a multi-million-dollar contract, an in-person interview with someone hard to connect with or climbing up a mountain. If you do not ask, then your answer will always be no. You should always ask for the business, meeting, or sale. If you do not try, it will not happen. If you do not seek, you will not find. Greatness does not happen without effort.

How do we do persevere effectively?

While not an exhaustive list, the following are some steps I believe we can take.

Break Down the Problem

Take care of what can be controlled and acknowledge elements of the situation that cannot. We can get easily overwhelmed by all the tasks in front of us that need to be accomplished. We put a sales plan together for a season or a year, and it may grow to seem insurmountable. Getting caught in trying to figure out how everything is going to be done can slow you down. Instead, think about the next most important item that you and your team can do to achieve the overall goal. At a conference once, one of the speakers provided a great acronym with the word, "W.I.N." If you want to win, focus on "**W**hat's **I**mportant **N**ow." Simplify your situation as much as possible and seek to take the next most important step.

We should also be mindful that there are some aspects we simply will be unable to control. We cannot control the weather, economic conditions, how people will react, or physical limitations. It has been said that life is 5 percent what happens to you and 95 percent how you respond. Break down and deal with what you can control. Understand and acknowledge the areas you cannot. Leverage what you believe is a setback or disadvantage in a positive way. Ask, "What can I do with what I have?" rather than stating, "I will never be able to do anything because of what I do not have."

Make a Plan

It's commonly said, "If you fail to plan, you plan to fail." A lot of people like to blaze the trail forward or build the plane while it is going down the runway. Sometimes we do have to be adaptive in the moment and adjust as we go. However, when we feel overwhelmed, it's helpful to create an outline or a framework around our perseverance. If you climb a tall mountain, it's good to know where your next checkpoint is so you can plan accordingly.

Alex Honnold is undoubtably one of the most famous and best free solo climbers in the world. Free soloing is done without any support or assistance other than your hands, shoes, and chalk. One of his most notable climbs was the 3000-foot ascent of El Capitan in Yosemite National Park. Years earlier, without telling anyone he was doing it, Honnold free soloed Moonlight Buttress in Zion National Park. At one hour and twenty-three minutes, not only was it a speed record, but it was also a feat no one had attempted before.

Honnold said, "For me free soloing a big wall is all about preparation. In a real sense, I had performed the hard work of Moonlight Buttress the days leading up to the climb. Once I was on the route, it was just a matter of executing."[2] Honnold could see in his mind all the steps along the way he would need to take and how they would be faced. For us, this speaks to the importance of planning and preparation before we take on challenges.

Engagement With People Who Can Help

Many people want to do everything on their own. They want to be the lone wolf and forge the path ahead solely on their own power. As much as possible, I am the kind of person who does this. However, as we go along the path toward success, we will sometimes not be able to do this. Even Alex Honnold, when he is not free soloing, trains and works with others. Some may say they do not want to owe anything to anyone. For others it may be just an unspoken or unrecognized issue of pride. The reality is that limitations with knowledge, connections, and time will force you to rely on the assistance of others. We should be willing to be open to asking others for help. Just like asking for the business, a meeting, or sale, we should be willing to ask people we know (or don't know) for their help. I do not believe that people see this as a sign of weakness when approached from a position of genuine humility. Rather, I think those around you will see it as a sign of strength. It is when the requests are approached with a selfish ulterior motive that the façade of humbleness erodes and washes away over time.

I recognize that with sales there must be a lot of self-drivenness to achieve goals. However, I also acknowledge and am mindful that I cannot be successful without the team around me, helping follow through on what's being sold. It takes everyone working together to get from sales to success.

Take a Mental Position

Years ago, I decided that I would no longer watch scary horror movies. Some people can handle these types of films, shows, and events more than others. For me personally, I did not like seeing the images, and I did not like the way I felt afterward. I told myself, "No more of that!" I like to sleep at night. There is a lot of power, I believe, when we look at ourselves in the mirror and give ourselves a command, when we put a mental stake in the ground to do or not do something. People who effectively persevere tell themselves resolutely that they will not give up no matter how hard it gets.

David Goggins, the former Navy SEAL and ultramarathoner showcases this in his book, *Can't Hurt Me*. One of the ways he kept himself accountable was by setting goals and putting them on what he calls the "Accountability Mirror." Goggins challenges, "Write all your insecurities, dreams, and goals on Post-Its and tag up your mirror. Whatever your goal, you'll need to hold yourself accountable for the small steps it will take to get there. Self-improvement takes dedication and self-discipline."[3]

By putting these notes around the mirror and reminding yourself every day of what needs to be accomplished, you put mental stakes in the ground. What gets focused on will get done. Your mind will help you find a way—if your heart is seeking the desired outcome as well.

Pivot When Needed

There is a difference between circumstances that are difficult or challenging and ones that are fruitless. By fruitless I mean there ceases to be an opportunity for growth or gain down the road you're traveling. The more effective we become with sales, the more we grow in discernment if the well has run dry, or will run dry, on a given project or situation. This could be for any number of reasons. It could be that the prospect we are talking to no longer has decision-making authority. It could be because of economic or company conditions outside your control. It could be that the other party is being untruthful or unethical. If the relationship is steering you away from your mission, vision, and values, then it is wise to part ways. For all these reasons and more, it is important to know when to pivot away.

Be on guard against people and situations that are not yielding much for the time invested. Maybe the prospects are slow to be responsive, lining up the meeting is taking forever, or doors keep shutting on you. Know when to keep knocking. If one door after another does not work, see if you can find an open window to climb through. For me, I have typically tried many combinations of calling, emailing, social media messaging, adding to distribution lists, or seeking people at events. If there continues to be zero reciprocal response, then it is probably time to move on.

Push Forward, Keep Going

If you have collectively made a plan that you are working on, the going is most likely going to get tough. Be prepared to tell yourself to keep pushing forward. You may or may not be familiar with the Bible. There is a chapter in the Gospel of Luke that illustrates this well. Luke was not one of the twelve disciples, but he was a follower of Jesus. He was also a physician by trade, which I am sure everyone who traveled together at that time greatly appreciated. How many of you have said, "I wish we had a doctor in the family!" Luke's historical account gives us his observations and recordings from the life of Jesus on earth. In chapter 18 we read several parables (another name for stories) and teachings that Jesus is trying to impart on his followers.

It kicks off with him saying, "Now he told them a parable on the need for them to pray always and *not give up*" (18:1, emphasis added). In another version it says, "not lose heart." Right away Jesus is communicating to stay steadfast and keep going when the going gets tough. He continues in verse two and says there was a town with a judge "who didn't fear God or respect people." Also, in that town there was a widow who kept coming to the judge, asking for justice against an adversary. We do not know who the adversary was or what the widow was dealing with, but she kept going to the judge for justice. So, what happened next?

"For a while [the judge] was unwilling, but later he said to himself, 'Even though I don't fear God or respect people, *yet because this widow keeps persisting me, I will give her justice*, so that she doesn't wear me out by her persistent coming'" (Luke 18:4–5, emphasis added).

Here we have a judge who does not care about God, and he really does not care about people. But he is persuaded by persistence. That persistence is driven by the faith of a woman who believes that if she keeps going and does not give up that she will eventually receive justice. Then Jesus asks, "When the Son of Man comes [speaking of himself], "will he find faith on earth?" (18:7). Faith is belief in what has not happened yet, trusting that it will come to pass. For people of faith, it is seeing God keep His promises and not trusting a world around that is pushing discouragement, fear, and worry around us.

Soon after Jesus communicates the story of the widow, he illustrates persistence and faith in a real-time situation. Luke notes they were on their way to Jericho with a big crowd of people following them. Along the road was a blind man begging. This blind beggar heard the commotion and asked someone if they could tell him what was going on. They said Jesus was coming by.

> So he called out, "Jesus, Son of David, have mercy on me!" Then those in front told him to be quiet, but *he kept crying out all the more,* "Son of David, have mercy on me."
>
> Jesus stopped and commanded that he be brought to him. When he came closer, he asked him, "What do you want me to do for you?"
>
> "Lord," he said, "I want to see."
>
> "Receive your sight." Jesus told him. "Your faith has saved you." (Luke 18:35–41, emphasis added)

The beggar could have easily kept quiet because of the people around him. Yet he showed persistence.

What do you want to happen in your life? What are you trying to achieve? Are people telling you in some sense to be quiet? Are people that do not respect you saying to back off and go away? If you believe in God, what do you want Him to do for you? Are you reaching out? Are you hanging in there? Are you staying faithful?

The finish line may be just around the corner. The next sales contract could be one call or connection away. Do not give up on yourself. Do not give up.

Keep persisting and believing.

When All Else Fails

There are times when you may have tried everything, yet you are still in a place of discouragement and despair. The light at the end of the tunnel is not getting any brighter, or you may not see the end in sight at all. It is in these times when we feel like giving up that we have an opportunity to give of ourselves. This simply means giving our time to serve someone else. This could be volunteering with a local organization or charity. It could be as simple as doing a nice chore for a neighbor like taking their garbage cans out and back.

When we give of ourselves, it takes the focus away from our inward self. Our gaze will begin to focus outward. When we serve others in need out of kindness and goodness, we open ourselves up to different perspectives. Suddenly, persevering against what we face may seem less troubling and insurmountable. Again, before you give up, seek to give of yourself to others.

Did you know that the word "sell" actually originated from the Norwegian word, *selje*. This is not to be confused with the word, "selfie," where you take a picture of yourself. No, *selje* essentially means, "to serve." How many of us would do better selling a product or our character to others if we sought first the interest of others. What would benefit and serve them in the most meaningful way?

Serving and selling should go hand in hand.

Do Whatever It Takes

Coakley and my grandfather survived that difficult season, as hard as it was. They ended up losing approximately 60 percent of their estate. They spent twenty months in bankruptcy and around $1.8 million on attorney and accounting fees. My grandfather was seventy and Coakley was sixty-eight years old when they finally emerged from that mess. According to them, they came out of it all "leaner and meaner." There was another time of difficulty for these guys before that financial crisis they experienced. It is a story about perseverance and how our family got into the hotel business.

The year was 1964; Fred and Neil were flying around the Washington, DC, beltway in a helicopter. They spotted a plot of land in Lanham, Maryland, located within Prince Georges County. The feasibility study indicated that the highest and best use for the location would be a hotel.

Their intention was to build the hotel and hire an operator to be a partner in the project. Initially, they were looking at a Holiday Inn franchise and ended up getting connected to Roy Winegardner, who had developed several of them. Everything was progressing well, and plans were to move ahead with a partnership with Winegardner's company. The average room rate back then for underwriting purposes was placed at $14.00 per night.

Times have really changed.

My grandfather and his partner got the loan they were looking for, but right before they signed, someone in their office suggested that they could get a better loan elsewhere. They backed away from what they had on the table, which was a big mistake. Within two weeks the Federal Reserve Bank raised interest rates on commercial loans, and everything broke down. My grandfather and Neil Coakley ended up losing the Holiday Inn franchise and held the property for five years. Eventually they were able to secure a new franchise with Ramada Inn. They also connected with a new operator/investor, whom I'll call Bill, who was based out of the Midwest. This group would provide the management and the funding needed for all the furniture, fixtures, and equipment. After so much time had passed, they were finally able to get a construction and permanent loan to start the project.

My grandfather quickly realized that once they started clearing the land, the property they were building was right in the middle of a spring-fed swamp. One of the first bulldozers almost disappeared beneath the mud! Because of how saturated the ground was, a channel had to be built to make sure the land was properly drained. The property eventually celebrated its grand opening in November 1970. This was the first hotel to open on the beltway in Prince Georges County, Maryland.

The management company supplied all key staff members for the hotel. The property started off doing well but after about three months Bill started calling Fred and Neil, asking for additional funds. My grandfather and Coakley could not understand why this would be, so they started digging into the operations. They found out that Bill and the general manager were providing complimentary rooms for unknown people. And alcohol was being generously given to staff members and their friends. One day Bill said he was sick of his management being questioned, so he asked for a meeting. Everyone met in the penthouse suite at the property, and Bill stated that he would either buy out Neil and Fred's ownership, or they would buy him out. If they bought him out, they would need to pay for all the furniture, fixtures, and equipment. This came out to be around $450,000 if they wanted to regain 100 percent ownership of the hotel.

My grandfather asked if they could have a moment to step outside to talk it over. The way the story goes is that Fred told Neil, "Let's buy him out." Coakley replied, "We don't have any money, how can we do that?" Fred said, "Let's buy some time from Bill, and we'll find the money somehow." So, they went back in and told Bill that they'd buy him out in sixty days. If they didn't have the money by then, they would walk away. It turned out they were able to get another loan that they had to sign personally, but it worked. They closed on the loan July 1, 1971. The next morning when they arrived at the hotel, Bill had taken all the key staff members with him.

My grandfather explains it best in his personal journal:

> Neil took over at the front desk, and I headed for the kitchen. The skeleton crew was doing okay keeping the coffee going, but when someone ordered Eggs Benedict, they were stumped. I quickly got out the recipe books in the chef's office and looked up how to make this dish. When it talked about Hollandaise sauce, I really drew a blank. I didn't know this stuff had to stay heated on the stove for a good while until it got the right consistency. We served it on the eggs when it got warm. When the customer started on his Eggs Benedict, he wasn't too happy, and they let us know about it. I forgot how we solved that problem.

> There were a lot of problems for a week or so until we got enough talent on board to run the hotel properly.[4]

Eventually, my grandfather and Coakley found a new manager, but this individual also ended up stealing from them. Once that person was gone, then everything started improving. They became experts in hotel management and in one year received the award for "Best Hotel in the Chain" as well as the award for "Most Improved." After their success in Lanham, they were led to their next hotel project. This one would become one of the first Hilton franchises in the system.

The risks that my grandfather and his partner took along with perseverance displayed through the trials created huge blessings for our mutual families. Not just monetary blessing but also lessons learned. They could have easily given up, thrown in the towel, and moved on. But they did not do this. Their willingness to deal with hard circumstances stayed with them throughout their careers and personal lives. It stands as a reminder for me to not give up and to keep persevering. I hope it does for you as well.

Keep reaching and seeking and persevering.

You may not be known or recognized while you persevere; however, you will eventually be known and remembered for your perseverance. After the blind man receives his sight, Luke 18:43 says, "All the people, when they saw it, gave praise to God."

Your faith and persistence will not only help you, but it also has an opportunity to grow and flourish in the lives of others.

Keep going.

Ideas

Be Careful with Gimmicks

The product of that conference in DC that those people used to buy stocks is truly the only thing I remember about the event. If you are selling in life, you certainly want to be persuasive and creative with how you market. However, if what you do does not get any buy in, then what is the point? I would caution that you are not disingenuous with your approach. Be careful of gimmicks and tricks that harm others versus help them.

A guy once pulled up to our house when we were living in Florida. He had a big truck with a big white cooler in the truck bed. He said he was selling meat. I do not remember his pitch. I do remember that I ended up buying many boxes of frozen meat. I suppose this would not have been so bad except the product was not very good, and there was way too much of it. I ended up with buyer's remorse and vowed I would never do that again. We decided at this time that it would be good to put our dog on an all-chicken diet. She was an American yellow lab, and we fed her the frozen chicken breasts we purchased from the meat man. She got super skinny as a result. Friends and family thought something was wrong with her. We quickly ended that and got her back on regular dog food.

I cannot say whether the man was intentionally disingenuous or not. But staying true to building strong character traits within yourself will help fight the temptation to deceive others. Conversely, great character will help you persist in selling to others in the most upstanding way possible. That in turn builds customers for life and trust that is very hard to break.

Re-till the Soil

There are a lot of sales leads that after a while go seemingly dead and fall away from being top of mind. I periodically like to do what I call "re-tilling the soil." Re-tilling the soil is when you go back every so often to old leads and contacts to check in with them to see how they are doing. You never know what seed may start to grow from those efforts. Did you know that Bermuda grass can go up to eight weeks without water? When this happens, the grass goes dormant and looks as if it could never be revived. However, once it's sufficiently watered, it turns green again. Find old leads to re-till and put water on them again. If nothing else, your prospect should appreciate your continued persistence.

Go Down the Road a Little

I think there is an element of perseverance that comes alongside our ability to take risks. We should not be quick to walk away from every opportunity because at first glance it does not feel like it will go anywhere. We should be willing to take risks to go down the road a bit so we can peek around the corner. Over the years I have come across projects and opportunities that did not ultimately mesh well with our business model. Their property condition was bad and with no hope of restoration, location was inaccessible, fees for service too small, and so on. Yet others did not seem great at first, but ultimately, they proved to be worth going down the road.

Questions to Consider

- What is a challenge that you can look back on where you felt that it was successfully navigated?
- What worked and what did not work?
- What is a challenge that you are dealing with right now? Have you told anyone about it?

I do not think that there is any other quality so essential
o success of any kind as the quality of perseverance.
It overcomes almost everything, even nature.
—John D. Rockefeller

Your Takeaways

I hope there was a learning lesson for you from reading about perseverance. What are one or two things you want to remember? Take a moment to write those thoughts out here: ______________________

CHAPTER 7

Communication and Building Relationships

If one plan won't do, then another must.
—John A. Roebling, *The Great Bridge*

As the American Civil War moved further away in history's rearview mirror, growth and industrialism continued to rise in America. Specific areas of prominence furthered their economic expansion with increases in population, commerce, and sales of all kinds. The cities of New York and Brooklyn were among these areas. They had become two of the largest cities in the country during the mid-1800s. With their size continuing to swell on either side of the East River, the desire for a connection between the two metropolises did as well. The solution was obvious. The idea of a bridge between these pieces of land was on the minds of many citizens dating back to the turn of the century. The bigger overarching question, of course, was how it could possibly be done and who could possibly make it a reality. The answer was found in a man by the name of John A. Roebling.

German born John A. Roebling was in his late sixties by early 1869 and was an engineering genius when it came to the construction of bridges. Despite his acclaim, those in political, financial and engineering circles all had doubts that he could make it happen. The engineering community called it a crazy idea. As his plan came together, he had to convince investors, backers, experts, consultants, and others that his plan would be the one to succeed. He had to sell them on his plan and on himself. "Roebling had assembled his seven consultants and with total patience and candor went over everything with them point by point."[1] At this time in history, it was to be the largest suspension bridge in the world. The Washington Monument had yet to be completed and thus the bridge, if it were to be finished, would also be one of the largest structures built in North America.

He meticulously walked through how everything would be accomplished. Then Roebling took respective individuals who would be backing the bridge project to locations where his prior work had been completed. "The Bridge Party," as it was known, visited bridges in Niagara Falls, Cincinnati, and Pittsburgh. At the end of the tour, experts and contributors had little remaining doubt that his plan would be successful.[3] It was not long after work commenced that Roebling had an unfortunate accident that ultimately led to his death. Roebling's son, Washington Roebling, was the most qualified to carry the project forward, and he did just that. The work was harder than imagined and was not without ongoing setbacks and challenges. The bridge finally opened on May 24, 1883, with his wife, Emily Roebling, completing the first official trip across. It took approximately fourteen years to complete all the work, and it still stands today: the Brooklyn Bridge. The origination of this wonder of the world began with the thorough communication and the experience of John Roebling.

Communication is all about building bridges, connecting one person or group of people to another. Everyone, whether they admit it or not, has a desire to feel heard, be connected, and to have expectations met. There is an innate desire in everyone for stable relationships with friends, coworkers, family members, neighbors, and people in general. We were built for connecting and connections. When it comes to sales and selling in life, building bridges of communication within relationships is one of the most important ongoing, never-ending actions we must pursue. And if you do not build them, then someone else will.

What does this mean? Communication is not just about being able to get up in front of a group of people to give a speech. Public speaking is certainly important. You need to be able to articulate thoughts and ideas in a manner that can capture attention to trigger a desired audience response. However, being an effective communicator goes beyond talking in front of others. It is all encompassing. It is the ability to proactively see beyond the moment, knowing what to say or send in advance. It is knowing when to pause to collect your thoughts before responding. At certain times silence can be equally, if not more, important than speaking. It is following through on what needs to be said and shared with another party, so they are not left in the dark. It can also be words that need to be said despite how painful they may be to say. Communication is setting boundaries and expectations so others know what they can or cannot do. It is thinking ahead so that you and others can be better prepared. Perhaps most of all, effective communication is about being a good listener. When you listen and are present in the moment, you will be more able to respond and attend to what has been communicated both verbally and nonverbally.

There are many facets to this subject. If you search for books on communication just on Amazon, you will come up with over 70,000 potential results. Mastering all techniques and aspects will be a lifelong, never-ending process. At the time of this writing, I have been married for over nineteen years, and I am still trying to be a better communicator with my wife. I still make mistakes when communicating with different team members, clients, prospects, friends, and family. My goal is to keep progressing, and I hope you will as well. Let's go through some areas of communication to just scratch the surface of this subject.

Who I Am Communicates to Others— One Way or Another

The Disney College program I previously mentioned is basically an internship where Disney brings down and trains new cast members for different positions. We stayed for a period of a few months between semesters. During that time, we also had an opportunity to take Disney leadership classes with our peers. It was a great experience, and I took a class that worked through the Meyers-Briggs personality test. Over the years since then I have done DISC, color tests, and all sorts of assessments to get a better understanding of my personality traits. Perhaps you have taken some of these tests as well. Why have so many people created these different assessments anyway? So that we can know ourselves better, of course. Beyond knowing more about ourselves, doing these tests teaches us to see specific traits in others. This is so we can know how best to interact and communicate with different people.

If you have a better understanding of how certain people respond to different types of communication, then you can be more effective at selling and leading. Some individuals will get captivated by numbers, charts, and figures. Others will want to hear stories and all about how great they are. Some want meticulous details, and others want broad, high-level discussion. Everyone is different, and the more we can recognize these differences or preferences, the better we will be able to appeal to them. My grandfather was more of a back-of-the-napkin kind of guy. He wanted to see the high-level picture. His partner on the other hand wanted all those meticulous details in big, thick binders. Some are more technical and want to hear about the functions and nuances of your product or experience. Others are more creative and want to hear about the possibilities and dream about all the what ifs. Some prospects prefer the phone, while others prefer email or text. You want to be able to know yourself and then be able to read others so that you can communicate in the best possible way.

Building Bridges to Others

We have talked about how communication is like building bridges. One nuance to this is connecting other people together who you feel will mutually benefit from meeting one another. This is literally building bridges to people, and it is honestly one of my favorite parts of selling. I was at a meeting where someone said, "If Mark is introducing us to you, we knew we would have to meet because it would be a good connection." That's the kind of person and place you want to be, and it comes back to listening, building trust, being intentional, and seeking out the best for others. I have always made it a point to seek out the best for any project. The best for that project may mean that our company or I do not end up getting the business. I've often said that famous axiom of life that "what goes around comes around." The goal is for the prospect or client to be successful at the end of the day. If you and I keep seeking that outcome as well, I know we will be successful in return.

A question for all of us is whether we are *bridge builder*s or *barrier makers*?

A bridge builder puts others first before themselves. A barrier maker stifles communication from going back and forth. They are the ones who make it difficult for relationships to grow and flourish. Most of us tend to build walls versus bridges. How do we overcome this to make the paths between others more seamless and plentiful?

Seek to Approach Life and Sales with a Sense of Humility and a Willingness to Learn.

We were once managing a small boutique property in the Southeast. It was a neat little retro hotel very close to the beach and had several owners representing it that we worked for. The property was in a tough labor area. This means it was difficult to find and retain talent throughout the year. One of the owners of the property developed an obsession with one of our maintenance workers at the hotel. The obsession was all about getting rid of him. This owner believed in their mind that the individual was not doing his job, and they went to great lengths to prove it. The owner would stalk the maintenance worker, watching him from their car throughout the day. The owner would tell us what he was wearing while working in the heat of summer.

This owner concluded that the maintenance worker needed to be terminated. We understand that some clients may want specific team members terminated for different reasons. There is a process by which this should be handled, and we explained the best way to go about it. The obsession became a vendetta against this worker. Our owner would not listen to our advice and suggestions. Their obsession clouded out any willingness to learn and listen from the professionals they had hired to manage the property. This owner wanted the worker to be gone at all costs. The conversations between them and our team were draining and wasteful. This team member was unfortunately let go in a manner that we did not approve of.

You cannot let yourself get so focused and narrowed in on something, or someone, where you ignore reason, logic, and understanding. We are all salespeople, and those looking to develop a strong character.

Therefore, we should approach business and life with a sense of humility and willingness to continually learn and grow ourselves. If you do not do this, eventually you and I will be left behind or make severe mistakes. Over the course of selling our company's services, I admit I have not had all the answers. The longer I have been in hospitality, the more I see things I did not expect to. You will not always know the answer to everything as well. Be willing to admit this to your client or prospect. You should also be willing to admit this to your friends and family. Find the people or resources who can give you the answer. The longer you live, the more you will learn and grow from mutifaceted people and situations. This is simply a matter of time and experience. Yet time and experience can easily be squandered. Great learning lessons can be pushed to the side and forgotten.

Do not waste difficult and challenging situations.

A challenge for some is the ability to check their ego at the door. I can honestly say that if I had not swallowed my pride many times over the years, it would have spelled disaster for our company. There are times when you, as the salesperson and the leader, need to stand up for what is right. This does not mean that you need to be right all the time. Do not be the person who is a know-it-all. How often have you been around individuals like this and cannot wait to get away from them? Seek to be a life-long learner, be a listener, look for opportunities to serve and put others before yourself. One of the values for our company is "the greatest leaders are the greatest servants." I would say the same is true for those in sales and those seeking to build a stronger character. In any walk of life, if you have a willingness to serve and put others first, you will without a doubt stand out in a sea of people.

Be the First to Forgive

A further point along the lines of effective communication and humility is a willingness to forgive others. Nothing will stifle communication, put up barriers, or squash relationships quite like the inability to forgive. As we progress through our days, there will be plenty of moments where we feel others have done us wrong. I get that the situation or experience you may be thinking of right now was probably awful. However, I am willing to bet that what you have experienced is not totally unique. Through the course of business, I have been lied to, stolen from, cheated, stabbed in the back (figuratively), yelled at, and had my faith thrown in my face. I do not have to forget any of these moments, but I have the opportunity to forgive those individuals and move forward. If I don't, unforgiveness locks me in a personal prison—which inflicts a worse punishment on me than the original offense. The same can be true for you, which is not what you want.

The longer you and I hold on to whatever we feel has wronged us in the past, the longer we will be trapped by it. There is freedom that comes with forgiveness. Successful relationships are not built by people and teams that hold grudges and count the wrongs. Selling is about building relationships. How many times have you heard it said, especially when it comes to sales, that you never want to burn bridges. You never know how paths are going to cross again in the future. I cannot count how many times I have said, "You know, it really is a small world after all." Keep the lines of communication open and together.

Be the first to forgive.

Show Care and Follow-up

Those who are effective at sales and communication make it happen because I believe they genuinely care. They care beyond the transaction because they are seeking to build excellence within themselves and their organization. We once had an opportunity to manage an incredible iconic location in South Florida. Our company was up against a couple groups for the contract, and we ultimately got the deal. I believe the owners chose us partly for our experience and because they could see we were a company that cared. Experience may get you the signature, but care and communication help keep the relationship.

A few months after we got the deal signed, this same property was to be transitioned under our management. We were getting down to a couple of weeks before the transition between our company and the one that was leaving. Typically, before this happens, you start to change over accounts and systems. One of the big items to transfer is insurance. This includes your property and general liability coverage. We found out that for about a month or so the property had zero liability insurance in place. This is not a good thing. As a business you do not want to go a day without liability insurance because anything can happen at any time. This is especially true for a hotel property. Without insurance you are leaving yourself vulnerable to claims that could sink you. When it comes to the hotel business, if it can happen, it will happen.

I may have been the one in sales to get the deal done, but I took it upon myself to do everything I could to get insurance in place. This was both before and after the property came under our management oversight. I contacted the prior company and was able to get the coverage backdated to the time it had dropped off months before. We were able to get everything set up and in place by the time we started. All along the way I was continually updating our clients with the status and progression of where we were with everything. Was it a part of my role and responsibilities to do any of these actions? No. I could have easily said, "That's not my job," and left it for someone else to deal with. No one could have done anything, and some unfortunate circumstance may have happened.

One of the worst statements we can make is, "That's not my job." If we have within ourselves the capacity to assist our team, we should always lean in where we can. If we are in sales and selling ourselves, then care and concern must go beyond our position and job description.

When clients and people experience caring in action, it builds a foundation of trust that is not easily swayed. I once had a guy come to our door looking to sell pest control services for our home. He walked me through everything they do and offer. He was pushy. I explained we were happy with our current company but told him that he could leave me his card. He said he did not want to give me his card. He was not even willing to do that, and I never saw him again. We built no lasting foundation during our interaction, which left no possibilities for changes that may have happened in the future. In our South Florida project, our clients saw the effort and care that I had before the contract officially started. I believe that this really stuck with them. The same can be true for you and your team. However, if no one else stands up, then it must be you who fills the gaps in care and communication.

Be Authentic and Dependable

In the movie *Aladdin*, Aladdin asks the genie for dating advice. The genie suggests that he be himself and tell the truth to Jasmine about not being a prince. Aladdin does not listen to the genie or the bee version of his magical friend. The result backfires in a big way. In the end Aladdin gets where he wants to go, but the journey there could have gone a lot easier.[5] Why do we tend to fear telling the truth and be ourselves? It's said that when you tell the truth, you do not need to remember what you say, but if you lie, you'd better have a good memory. I think we should try to remember what we say, but we certainly do not need to be aware of all the details.

Many sales programs and teachers talk about the importance of being authentic. Yet even though this is highlighted, not many in business fully get it. We as consumers tend to go back to the people and companies we trust. We go back to places where we feel people are being genuinely honest with us. I appreciate, as I'm sure you do, when a doctor, dentist, car mechanic, contractor, banker, or whoever tells me what I need and what I do not need. Likewise, I have always wanted to be straightforward with the prospective clients I have interacted with. I tell them that I want to work together but only if it makes sense. In the hotel world, if we do not get a sense that we will be successful with the property and the overall business relationship, it is important to communicate that up front. You do not want to go into a situation where you know it is not going to work out.

Who you are on Monday morning should match who you are throughout the rest of the week. That includes in and out of work. Why do we tend to give our best to the people at work but end up giving the least to the people we love at home? I say this as a challenge to myself just as much as I am saying this to you. Authenticity starts behind closed doors where no one else can see and it is carried out throughout all situations. Someone with high integrity probably correlates with someone who you can sense is genuinely authentic. The word integrity is derived from the word "integer." This basically means a whole number. Wholeness or completeness is a great way to view authenticity. Who you are on Monday should be the same person you are on Saturday night or Sunday morning.

It goes without saying that honesty and strong moral ethics are built within this as well. Sales may take off through dishonest means, but it will not be sustainable. Tell people what they need to hear, not what they want to hear. Share what aspects of your product will be most helpful to them for improving their lives. Be upfront about whether your product, service, or idea will be right for them.

Be honest.

When you admit what you do not know, you build trust with people. How you respond when you lack specific knowledge and understanding with others is important. My brother-in-law, Mike, went through a challenging time when he ended up needing a liver transplant. Mike shared some reflections on this time with me.

He said, "When I think about admitting when I do not know something and being honest, it reminds me of how my doctor communicated with me. My liver doctor would say, 'I actually don't know the answer to your question, but I will find out and get back to you.' He always did this within a day or two and would often call me on Fridays at 8 p.m. on his way home. This made me believe what he told me more because he would admit when he didn't know something. This was a guy I trusted with my life. The stakes were high. I did not need him to know everything immediately; I did need him to use the access he had to knowledge and other people to find the answers. This built trust for me, in a time when I was most critical of professionals. Certainly, this applies to sales. You also have access to knowledge and people along with the ability to find answers. Building trust with what you know comes with time and experience. It shows self-confidence by being honest and admitting what you don't know."

Bridges are built in life and sales with authenticity and integrity. One more thing: If you say you are going to do something, follow through and make it happen. People are drawn to dependability. When you follow through on the commitments you make and deadlines you set, it creates layers of trust. There have been a couple times I have had clients sign our agreements without even reading them. I am not suggesting this as something everyone should do. However, those types of situations only occur when trust is established, and people are confident they can depend on you and your team.

Positivity and Encouragement

Situated in the Elk Mountain Range approximately twelve miles southwest of Aspen, Colorado, is one of the most photographed areas in the United States. Known for its shape and coloring when the light is just right, the Maroon Bells are a bucket list stop for travelers young and old. My family and I decided to walk around the lake that sits at the base of the mountain. We set off on what we thought was the trail. Since that experience, we have learned that it is wise to take a picture of the trail map prior to leaving.

Making our way along the path we quickly realized that we were not on the one we had originally thought. Rather, we were continuing to walk vertically without any idea of where we were going or how long it would take to get there—wherever "there" was. We also had nothing else with us except our thermoses full of water and our dog. We asked a couple of people who were walking nearby if they could provide any sense of direction. They said that the path we were on would eventually lead to another lake, and it would take about an hour to reach it. We asked if what we had with us would be enough. They encouraged us, saying, "You guys have everything you need to get there. You can do it!" We pressed on.

We occasionally asked those who were coming down how much farther we had to go. They would tell us approximately how much time and say we would get there eventually. After passing through a long boulder field, we finally made it up to Crater Lake. It was incredible and well worth the effort to get there. As we took some time to sit and relax, a couple ladies sat down near us. They chatted with us and petted our dog. One of them said out of nowhere to my wife and me that she could tell we were great parents. She encouraged us to keep going and that we were an inspiration for her and her young family. We were not expecting such kind words from a stranger.

As we go through life, there is power in an encouraging word isn't there? Everyone, regardless of age, status, position, or anything, all need it from time to time. When days get tough and we face situations where we do not know where we are going or how long it is going to take to get there, an encouraging word is refreshing. It lifts our spirits and gives the extra boost to keep going. Encouraging words do not create barriers, they always build bridges.

In the late nineties Ken Sutterfield wrote a little book, *The Power of an Encouraging Word*. Sutterfield tells short stories of how encouraging words and actions changed people's lives for the better. He says, "Words of encouragement are the most effective method of getting people to do their best."[3] It may not be just words. Sutterfield tells a story of Thomas

Jefferson. The former president was traveling with a group of people, and they eventually arrived at a riverbank that was swollen from heavy rains. Because the bridge was washed away, they had to cross with their horses. The threat and danger of being washed away was very real. A stranger asked the president if he would ferry him across. The president agreed and they made it to the other side. One of the travelers asked the stranger why he had asked the president to take him across. The man had no idea it was the president. He said, "All I know is that on some of your faces was written the answer no, and some faces was written the answer yes. His was a yes face."4 Do we exhibit a face of encouragement? Or not?

When we came down the mountain, we felt more positive. We found ourselves encouraging others who were making their way up. Encouragement from others, I believe, helps foster further encouragement. It is kind of like throwing a rock in a pond of still water. The ripple effects get larger and expand outward. In many areas of life, we must be self-driven, self-motivated, and act for ourselves. However, life itself is not meant to be taken on alone. It is by lifting one another up, sharing each other's burdens, and providing encouragement that strong relationships are forged, and the storms of life are weathered.

You may have never heard of three people named Stephanas, Fortunatus, Achaicus. These three gentlemen lived in Corinth around the year AD 56. The apostle Paul was wrapping up his first letter to the Corinthian Church and made it a point to highlight these individuals. Paul wrote, "I was glad when Stephanas, Fortunatus and Achaicus arrived, because they have supplied what was lacking from you. For *they refreshed my spirit and yours also.* Such men *deserve recognition*" (1 Corinthians 16:17–18, emphasis added).

Is there someone you can think of in your life who refreshes your spirit? We have the opportunity in our sales interactions and relationships to be spirit lifters, to be encouragers. Let us seek to be these types of individuals—but not for the purpose of getting recognition.

Rather, let us seek to do this for the purpose of building others up, which in turn has the power to lift our own spirit as well.

Perhaps in the process it can help break down barriers and build stronger bridges to others as well.

The Value of Serving Others

The South Florida property that we managed only stayed around for a couple years. The group that owned it ultimately decided to manage the property themselves. However, those early interactions in the beginning of showing care and communicating never left the minds of the owners. It was sad to say goodbye to this group of people.

We had another group that we have worked with for many years in the Mid-Atlantic that reciprocated care during the midst of the pandemic. The hotel industry was one of the hardest hit during the pandemic. As I have explained, hotel management company revenue is mainly comprised off a percentage of hotel total revenue. With the lack of guests staying in hotels, income for properties went way down. As a result, our revenue as a management company plummeted in 2020. Yet we continued to provide and maintain the same level of care and service that we had always provided. We just had to become more creative to accomplish it. The saying during this time was, "We are doing more with less."

Our one group of owners recognized that their operator was going through a difficult time. Then something amazing happened in a series of incredible miracles that occurred between March and April of 2020. These clients we worked with said they would be willing to continue to pay us the same amount in fees we typically would receive monthly. Why? Because as they told me, "We want you to succeed." Thinking about that moment, this many years later makes me want to cry. It sheds light on the power of relationships and building bridges instead of barriers.

Our client's offer was a huge blessing for us. They, as a business, were incredibly blessed throughout and beyond the pandemic. I do not believe that they have been blessed as owners because of what they did necessarily but rather because of the position of their hearts. They wanted to give of themselves so that another group could be lifted up.

Do you want to be a great salesperson? Then seek to serve and not to be served.

Do you want to be a great leader? Then seek to be a blessing for others and not to be blessed.

Do you want to grow strong character within you? Then watch the position of your heart.

Do you want to build bridges? Then do not build barriers between others.

Questions to Consider

- Who is someone you admire that is a good communicator?
- What do they do that makes you feel this way?
- Is there someone you feel you need to do a better job building a bridge of communication with?
- Who is that? And why?
- What can you start doing today to begin strengthening the relationship?
- Why is forgiveness so hard sometimes?
- Is there someone you need to stop and forgive today?

It's surprising how much you can accomplish
if you don't care who gets the credit.
—Abraham Lincoln

Your Takeaways

What is something that caught your attention from this chapter? Take a moment to write out what resonated to you. Is there an action item you would like to begin working on now toward communicating with others in a more effective way?

CHAPTER 8

A Path to Change

Success is to be measured not so much by the position
that one has reached in life
as by the obstacles which he has overcome while trying to succeed.
—Booker T. Washington

Between 2011–2012 our company struggled to pick up management contracts and connect with new clients. The struggle had been getting progressively harder prior to my stepping into the business development role for our company. I had been focusing on business development since late 2010. And as I mentioned, revenues for a hotel management company are derived predominantly from fees based off a percentage of hotel revenue. Typically, this is anywhere from 2.5 percent to 4 percent depending on the property. If the typical hotel does about three-to-four million in revenue, then you can easily calculate how much a management company will receive as their base fee.

Management groups must continually bring in new business or new management contracts to fuel the company engine. For our business in any given year, we would typically pick up three-to-four of these management contracts at the most. It is also typical for most companies that there is also churn, the occurrences when customers stop doing business with a company over a given period. Properties can leave a portfolio for a variety of reasons. We jokingly said sometimes that we could write a book called "101 ways to lose a contract." One of those ways we found was because of doing a great job! Most of the time, though, it is because clients sell their hotels. When this occurs, buyers of properties tend to bring in new management groups with them.

Unfortunately, more locations were leaving the pipeline during this period than filling it. I used to think that businesses had seasons. There would be periods when keeping everything intact became more difficult than others. I eventually realized it was not seasonal but rather an everyday reality. Running a business is sometimes like trying to hold sand in your hand. An old rotisserie oven commercial on TV had personality Ron Popeil put a chicken in the oven and say, "Just set it and forget it." While being a catchy slogan, this does not work with business. You cannot have a mentality of setting your business and forgetting it. We must always seek to improve and to take care of the customers we have. We must always seek the building of bridges to new relationships, business, and excellent team members.

For us at the time, none of the bigger projects we were working on seemed to be landing anywhere. Contrary to what I said earlier about not seeing failure as failure, at this point in my life I was taking failure hard and letting it weigh me down. There were a couple projects in these years that we worked hard to earn. One was a great potential project in South Florida. Get this, we were one of around a hundred management companies that the prospective client looked at. It was a very lengthy interview process. After tons of work and effort, the group whittled their choices from ten down to five, and then three. We finally ended at number two as the runner up. Why? They felt the other company had better connections within the hotel brand than we did.

Not Getting the Job

People have all sorts of reasoning and logic that help them filter through the selections and choices they ultimately make. This is not just for a management company selection but any purchase or partnership.

Believe it or not, we once had a prospective client flip a coin because he could not decide which company to go with. I can understand doing this if you are having a hard time picking an entree off a dinner menu. However, leaving the oversight of an investment worth millions of dollars totally up to chance does not make much sense to me. At any rate, in that case, we ended up on the winning side of the coin.

Along the way, in the interview process for the South Florida project, the prospective client had a consultant assisting with the management company selection. The group was comprised of foreign investors. They had an American contact who served as their liaison and interpreter. I'll call him Ted. He apparently had a background in business and hotels. We could tell the guy relished the control and power he had been given. As we were wrapping up our day, Ted asked a pointed question: "Do you guys think you could tone down the religious talk? It would be best if we kept God out of the conversations with this investment group." We asked in return if we had said something offensive to the principals of the investment group. He said no, but in reviewing our company video, website, newsletters, and values, he felt like the information we had would be off-putting to them. We told Ted that because we were a private company, we could include our values and beliefs in our communication material. We told him that we did not make people believe anything. We simply stated that our values come from our belief and trust in God. Our goal was to love, honor, and respect all people that we work with and serve.

Our explanation did not make a difference.

To almost cross the finish line on this sizeable South Florida opportunity only to come up short was a stinger. We would have been hurt in a season of plenty, but it hurt even more in this season of drought we were experiencing. While religious beliefs were not explicitly cited, this could have been the determining factor in the minds of the foreign group. Looking back now, if that was part of the decision-making process, then it's probably for the best that we did not end up working together.

We will not always line up perfectly with prospective or even current clients. That is not the way the world works. We are all human beings after all. As we enter any business relationship, we should desire to be a positive influence for all parties. Be a light. While it may not always be reciprocated, there should be at least mutual respect between both parties. Otherwise, any relationship, business or otherwise, will not see the longevity that I believe we all truly want in the end.

Another example that stands out to me was a project in Nebraska. It was a new construction property in a growing downtown market that we were excited about. We had never managed this brand before but got all the approvals and thumbs up from the franchise to do so if we were selected. Our team was excited and did an awesome job studying the market and putting together our plan for success. We had great meetings with this group as we toured the area and explained our capabilities. We put together several different iterations of projections that showed strong viability. We answered question after question from this prospective client in the hope that if we showed enough knowledge and expertise, we would earn the opportunity to manage and oversee this incredible hotel.

As time progressed, it felt like we were giving way too much information away. At one point, my father was even saying that we had to be careful about how much more information we provided. The prospective client could easily take all our thoughts and ideas and just not hire us. They could say, "Thanks for sharing everything. I don't need you anymore!" In a sense, that is exactly what ended up happening. When it finally came time to make the selection, we did not get the job opportunity because the gentleman felt that we would not be hands on enough. He figured that because we were a Maryland-based company, we would not have enough oversight of a property based in Nebraska.

For years we successfully operated properties in many states outside and away from our corporate office. In this case we could not crest the peak on the mountain of perception. In this man's mind, we just could not be hands-on enough because of our corporate office location. Today it is not uncommon to operate businesses from a distance. The key now, as it has always been for hotel management companies, is having a strong local property team in place that can be worked with from anywhere. Also having good systems, tools and procedures that can be utilized. Perhaps you and your business have been shut down for similar reasons. You were not close enough—or just the opposite, you were too close! You may have experienced this when trying to sell a group or individual on an idea. Some may look at you and say you do not have enough of something. That something could be money, education, or experience. When the other side shuts us down, it is easy to become discouraged and have a desire to throw in the towel. That is how I felt after this situation.

When this deal slipped through our grasp, it knocked me mentally. Our team was disappointed, and my headspace felt like it was stuck in mud. We put a lot of time and effort into getting this opportunity across the finish line. You have probably said to yourself at some point, "I don't know what else I or we could have possibly done to make this happen." Despite our experience and capabilities, we did not have an answer to win the day here. I was sick of losing and coming up short. And I felt that I was being taken advantage of.

A Mental Shift and Direction Shift

Losing out in Nebraska became a pivotal point in my life moving forward on how I would respond to success and failure. Maybe you have been there yourself. Stalled out at the mental fork in the road between progression and regression. My whole outlook on sales and selling in business would come to totally change. Just like I mentioned in Chapter 3, I would stop seeing failure as failure and losing as not gaining anything. I'd start seeing it as protection, getting closer to the right opportunity, building connections, learning, growing, and developing trust.

You can arrive at the same place as well. To continue forward, our mind needs to shift the lens through which our eyes see the world and circumstances. There are days and times in our life where we just cannot change that lens on our own power. We need to let a higher authority step in and take control. God had to open my eyes a little more before I could see everything that He wanted me to see. Perhaps even more importantly, respond in a way that would be honoring to Him.

To do this though, we must be willing to let go, which is easier said than done.

Battling Perceptions

I mentioned stories where our company did not get business for several reasons. Our company was too far away. Another group had stronger connections. Our head office was out of state. We had biblical values. Over the years I have battled against many different perceptions and versions of "no thanks." Just when you think you've heard it all, you'll hear something new. Statements like, "We do not feel like you are a fit because you have too many hotels in this market." "You can't because you don't have enough properties in a market." "You have not managed here as long as this other group." "You can't because you're too small." "You can't because you are too big." The list goes on and on. People are looking for all sorts of reasons to be able to justify why they do not like your company, you, or your idea.

It does not matter if you are a big or a small company. I know because I have worked for both. It does not matter if you are young, or you are old. I know because I have been young and sort of old. You will always have to overcome perceptions. How do we do our best to battle against them and give ourselves the best chance for success?

One of the best ways we can overcome negative perceptions, and "no" statements is to be prepared with our talking points or rebuttals that are coming our way. You will start to see and hear similar obstacles repeatedly. If, for example, someone feels your company is too small, how do you respond? You may say, "We are more flexible, adaptive, and responsive due to our size. We can be more hands on than other larger organizations." You need to determine and craft responses that you feel will resonate well. Point to stories of success when and where you can. They should also be truthful and honest.

You should also be confident in your response. We have talked about confidence already. When I was in college, I tried to get a job at the JW Marriott / Ritz-Carlton Grande Lakes property in Orlando, Florida. In addition to working at Disney, I wanted to be able to have Ritz-Carlton on my resume. At the time, the property was taking candidates through a screening process with a computer questionnaire and an over-the-phone interview. I tend to err on the side of being humble, and when asked how I would rank myself on a scale of one to ten, I probably said seven and a half to eight. I should have been more confident and said that I believed I was ten! In more words or less, I probably also told them that I would do any job they gave me. "I will clean the pool! Just let me in!" I guess these comments did not resonate well because I never received a call back. Desperation does not always work.

I believe the interviewees perceived that I was not confident in my skills and abilities, that I was not confident in myself. They wanted associates who viewed themselves as ten not as a middle-of-the-road team member. My wife on the other hand did get an opportunity to work at the Grande Lakes property. To this day, she still gives me a hard time about it.

At some point you may have done everything you could to overcome the reason why a prospective client, group, or person does not want to go with you. They may not even want to accept your free thirty-day trial. You provided confident and thoughtful responses to address their concerns. You may have even cited success stories of situations very similar to theirs. They could still say no. Here now is an important lesson in sales that I have learned: Trust that this "no" is for a reason and that you are on your way to your next "yes."

Balancing Both Your Time and How Much You Give

When I reflect on Nebraska, we could sense that we were giving up a lot of information to win that management opportunity. I always remind myself to be careful of putting all your eggs in one basket. Be cognizant of how much information you're giving away, and balance how much time you're spending on a specific project. You never want to neglect current clients who are happy and people that you care for. You do not want to pour all your energy and effort toward a prospect whom you have no idea will commit. Allocate time and energy to a variety of prospects. Some may take longer, but business will eventually be realized together. Then there are others who sign up relatively quickly. Fish where the fish are.

All of this takes experience to know how to have good time management skills. It does take time and experience to develop better discernment with when to know when you are being used versus where you should be allocating your most precious resources. You also want to line up the time you are allocating with prospects that make the most sense for your business or the dream you are trying to accomplish. Often, we would say that it takes just as much effort to gain and manage a small contract just as much as big one. Decide with your team on the most ideal scenarios that you are collectively seeking. Flex yourselves around that ideal scenario.

Finally, I would reiterate again that sometimes you should take conversations and connections down the road a bit. I have seen so often that what may appear to be not very worthwhile at first turn out to be a very good opportunity in the end. At the very least, if you are new to being in a sales position, it is a good opportunity to practice, learn, and grow. We once had the opportunity to manage a small property in a town on the outskirts of Austin. At first glance, given the size and location, it would not seem worthwhile to get involved with. We took it down the road and ended up having a long relationship with this client. Our company had the opportunity to manage other projects for this same group in other states and locations. Our willingness to see what was around the corner produced hundreds of thousands in fees for our business.

Ideas

Conference and Trade Show Set Up Effectiveness

When you or your company are exhibiting at a conference or tradeshow, do not sit down or behind a table. Be out in front and engage with trade show attendees as they are walking by. Be clear in your marketing materials what your company does. People tend to avoid making eye contact. Those walking by do not know yet that they need your service or product. Be willing to take some chances and try new ways to connect with individuals.

- Go up to speakers after they have completed a panel discussion and introduce yourself.
- Hand out a gift for a cup of a coffee with your company or name on it.
- Have good pre-and-post conference or event marketing.
- Pre-conference, try to identify as many attendees as possible in advance. Reach out and set up meetings with those you would like to connect with.

- Brainstorm with your team about ways you can engage and follow up.
- Keep attending large and small events so that you can continue practicing how to be effective at networking.

Take Notes and Share

When you are attending conferences, meetings, or events, seek to take notes of key takeaways you heard in different seminars and sessions. This becomes a nice follow up for you to share with your prospective clients or contacts. You can also share links to helpful/relevant online webinars, podcasts, or videos. I feel that when you share this information with current and prospective clients it is often well received.

Questions to Consider

- Has there been a time when someone turned you down or dismissed your idea or your business?
- What are some of the responses you have given to overcome those "no" obstacles they have thrown your way?
- Continual rejection can leave you discouraged and drained. What do you do or who do you go to for encouragement? It is important to fill ourselves up.
- Look at where you are allocating your time. Is there a particular area you feel you should cut back?
- Where do you need to say no so that you can say yes to something else?

Don't focus on what you think you deserve.
Take aim on what you are willing to earn!
—David Goggins, *Can't Hurt Me*

Your Takeaways

Has there been a time in your life where you have reached a mental fork on the road? What decisions did you make to keep going? Maybe you are in one of those seasons right now. Who do you need to reach out to now for guidance, wisdom, and direction?

CHAPTER 9

Circles

If you seek answers, you won't find them, but if you seek God, the answers will find you.
—Mark Batterson, *The Circle Maker*

It was an icy March night in Billund, Denmark, 1942. Everyone who was working for Ole Kirk Christiansen at the time was fast asleep. Christiansen, founder of O. Kirk Christiansen's Woodwork & Toy Factory, was the company that would eventually become known as Lego. He was a salesperson and a business owner who focused intently on delivering excellence in what his company produced. He was also someone who kept persevering despite continual setbacks and challenges. In its early days the company was riddled with continual problems. It seemed just when progress was being made, issues would pull them backward. In 1926 lightning struck the company's new workshop, and most of what they had been working on went up in flames. However, some of it was able to be salvaged. The previous workshop had burned to the ground as well. The following year, Christiansen fractured his skull due to an incident with a piece of machinery.

The company was also constantly in debt. The bartering and promises for paying creditors back seemed never ending. Christiansen's first wife had health issues and passed away. Sometime afterward he was about to file for bankruptcy. Then he met Sofie Jergensen, whom he eventually married. Sofie provided her savings, which allowed Christiansen to stay afloat a little while longer. World War II was in its early stages, and German occupation began to infiltrate Denmark. At one point German officers wanted to take over Christiansen's workshop and buildings for the purposes of barracks and storage. Thankfully, this did not end up happening. Then on that icy night in 1942 the company's new workshop caught fire again and completely burned to the ground.

Given everything that had happened up to this point, Ole Kirk Christiansen had every reason to allow despair, misery, and hopelessness to wash over him. While he doubted for the first time in a long while the plans God had for him, he nevertheless turned to his heavenly Father in prayer. Christiansen said, "As everyone knows, adversity is there to be overcome. It's through it that we humans are being refined. This was the third time I had to see my company burn to ashes. And this time it really was a big shock. I had to go to my bedroom to pray in my despair. Then I experienced something remarkable: the prayer became a thanks and a blessing for me. I was given invisible help. It was as though my difficulties were taken from me."[1]

From that point, Christiansen rallied the members of his team and rather than wallow in self-pity, he got to work. The company was able to build a brand-new factory, and business started to boom.

There is power in prayer.

The Circle Maker

Probably like Christiansen, I was tired of continuing to lose. About the time I was caught up in loss after loss while seeking business opportunities for our company, the pastor of National Christian Church in Washington, DC, Mark Batterson, released a book in 2011 called, *The Circle Maker.* Batterson sets up his book with the story of a first-century BC Jewish man named Honi, who prayed for rain. The land had been struck by a severe drought that threatened to destroy the people. Honi drew a circle in the dirt and swore to God that he would not leave that circle until mercy was shown on the land and its people. He prayed a prayer that only the God of the universe could answer. He prayed that rain would fall so bountifully that the drought would come to an end.

Batterson's book is all about praying boldly to God. God is not intimidated or overwhelmed by the burdens, dreams, concerns, challenges, or difficult prayers we have. As Batterson says, "Bold prayers honor God, and God honors bold prayers."[2] He wants you and me to bring them before Him. Drawing circles—whether figuratively or literally—draws attention and focus to the prayers where we need God to show up in a divine and miraculous way. It creates a lens of faith that we look through and puts a total dependence on the King of the Universe versus trusting completely in ourselves and others.

You may or may not have heard this before, but *God is for you.* He wants you to pray boldly to Him. One of the most amazing things I have seen over the course of my life is how He answers prayers. You may be able to say the same based on experiences you have had. They could be prayers for healing, wisdom, protection, gratefulness, or provision. These prayers always seem to be answered in unexpected ways that we could never have been planned or thought of on our own.

Draw Your Circle

Here is one such story.

My wife and I were in Florida at the time when *The Circle Maker* was released, and our church read through it in 2012. We were wrapping up reading through the book together when our efforts on the Nebraska project came to an end in failure. The New Year was approaching, and I felt something needed to change. I needed to start handing my position and efforts over to God. I decided I would circle a bold prayer that I knew only He could answer. At first, I thought I would pray for five hotels to come onboard in the coming year. However, I felt that God was bigger, and I was not being bold enough. Where I landed was circling a prayer that God would provide not five but ten new hotels for our family business in 2013.

You may think this number doesn't seem like a lot. And for me, many years down the road, transitioning ten properties now is not so much. The partnerships and hotels we have onboarded have been much more than that in some years. However, let me tell you, at that time bringing on that many properties within 365 days had never happened in the history of our company. In a typical year we would probably bring on three-to-four hotels at the most. This is also called transitioning a hotel. It is a lot of work to transition a property between onboarding new team members, systems, procedures, and stabilizing an asset. Hotel management companies are not in business because situations are perfect. Organizations such as ours are typically brought in to address problems, challenges, and issues. When you transition or onboard a hotel, you collectively tackle as many of these problems as possible at the very beginning. That does not mean that problems and issues do not continue to appear. You must adjust, pivot, and try new actions to get a location on more stable ground.

So, in that early time, I reached a point in my sales and business development role, and the history of our family company, where I was tired of not seeing opportunities happen. I have often asked in seasons of drought and little growth, "Why?" "Why is this happening? Am I personally not doing enough? Is there something we are missing as an organization? Are our competitors better or doing something different?"

For you in your sales role, you have probably come up against questions like this yourself. There have most likely been days when you have experienced discouragement and felt you are not doing enough as well. It may not be related to the organizational or company output that is expected. You may be asking why you have not been able to sell someone on a dream or idea that you have been working on for a while. Do not give up on yourself. Step back for a second and start connecting with someone who can help give wise direction and counsel. Start praying!

With sales and many aspects of life, we must frequently step away from forcing our own desired outcomes to happen and allow God's will to be done. Let Him lead the way. Like Honi, I began to prayerfully circle around a bold prayer to God that went something like, "God, I'm praying that in this year You would provide ten hotels for our business. I'm saying that number because the only way it can happen is if You are involved."

I not only prayed for this before the New Year but continued to do so throughout 2013. Keep in mind that our company had never picked up that many properties in a year. In fact, over the prior two years, 2012 and 2011, we had lost at least five hotels each year while picking up a few here and there. Acquiring ten new hotels wasn't just bold, it was a crazy prayer!

When approaching prayer, we should not liken God to a genie in a magic lamp that grants wishes whenever we want. If we do that, we will end up being disappointed. He is not in the business of granting wishes. He is, however, in the business of faith, hope, love, and transforming lives. He desires personal relationships with everyone, including you and me. As we read through Scripture, one of the aspects of humanity that Jesus marvels at is when people display unbridled faith in God. The Gospel of Luke chapter 7 tells a story about a centurion who asks for his servant to be healed.

One of the best definitions of faith I have heard is from Andy Stanley, senior pastor of North Point Community Church in Alpharetta, Georgia. He said one Sunday morning, "Faith is . . . 'God, I have confidence in you, and whatever you choose to do or not do, I have confidence in you. I don't have confidence in outcomes. I have confidence in the one that controls outcomes.'"[3]

I went into 2013 trusting God, the One who controls the outcomes, to answer my prayer however He determined was best. The answer could have meant we would have received fewer or no additional pieces of business. The way it would turn out was completely up to Him. I had faith that He would provide exactly what our company and I needed.

Ten Hotels Circled in Prayer

What happened with the ten hotels I circled in prayer? Probably the best way to explain what happened would be to share excerpts from a letter I wrote to the pastor of the church we attended. This would have been in December 2013 after a full year of praying boldly to God for ten properties. Here is what I wrote:

> Dear Robbie,
>
> I hope this message finds you well. The purpose of this message is perhaps to give us both some encouragement in the face of challenges we come up against. To tell you the truth, up to this point in my life I don't think that I had ever really prayed boldly before. I have always been solid with prayer. I am always very thankful, and I always ask God for a variety of things. But I haven't been bold. To the point where you step out in complete faith and challenge God to answer. As you

have also said many times, just because we ask for an oak tree doesn't mean we will always get one right away. He may give us an acorn to start with. That's kind of how my circle prayer progressed this year.

As January 2013 got started, we signed up to do a new construction project in New York—a deal I thought would never happen. I had been talking with that owner for over a year as he could never get the financing together to start the project. The financing miraculously came together for him, and more than that, the management company he was going to hire wasn't honest with him, so he switched back to us. The story of how the hotel got built was miraculous. Let's just say a mountain had to come down to make that happen. That's one.

A few days after I prayed the bold prayer for ten hotels in December, I placed a call to another guy I had been staying in touch with. This gentleman has a group of five hotels, four in the Washington, DC, area and one in Texas. I had been calling him for a year after he hired a close competitor of ours. I wanted to stay in touch and continue to see if he was satisfied with them or not. The day I called in December he asked when we could meet. Long story short, we finalized all the agreements to his five hotels in February and began operating all five hotels by April 1. I can't tell you enough how much of a big win this was and how miraculous it was at the same time. God had blown my mind, and the year had barely started. That's six total.

The next opportunity came with the acquisition of a property about an hour away from our corporate office in Hagerstown, Maryland. I met with the owner of this property about a year and a half ago. At that time, he couldn't afford us, so he hired an independent consultant instead. After working together for a while, the family decided to try to sell the hotel in 2013. They didn't get the price they were looking for and decided to bring on a management company to help continue to boost business and clean up hotel operations. He remembered us, and we started operating his hotel in May. That's seven.

In June one of our current clients hired us to operate their property in Pittsburgh. This has proven to be a difficult hotel for our group, but nevertheless this became number eight.

There are other ways for management companies to earn business. Sometimes this is through something called a receivership. Basically, when a hotel owner stops paying the mortgage payment on the hotel, the hotel loan and property is taken over by the bank (primary servicer). The bank then gives the duty of selling the hotel, recouping losses, and so forth to what is called a special servicer. The special servicer hires a receiver (management company) to come in and operate the property until it is ready to sell or something else. It turns out we got connected to one of the larger special servicers in the country. Bottom line is that over the course of June and July we were brought in to be the management company for three hotels located in Maryland and North Carolina. These three properties made eleven for the year. God answers prayer!

As the year 2013 progressed, we continued to work hard as a team, and more opportunities came along. We picked up a property in St. Petersburg, Florida, from an owner whose day job was in the jewelry business. I will never forget the multiple meetings I had with him in a mall food court after finding him at his jewelry store. All told, by the end of 2013 we had onboarded fourteen hotels in total! God answered prayer through the amount of provision that only He could make happen. He made it rain.

You may say that sounds incredible. Here is the really incredible part. As it happened, this year became a very challenging time for some of our properties. Our family owned a large full-service Hilton hotel in Virginia, not far from Washington, DC. It was a property my grandfather had built in 1978. Our company received a large number of fees from the management of this one hotel. Remember, we receive fees based off a percentage of the total revenue that is generated by the hotel. A strong portion of business for this property was generated from government contracts.

In 2013 the business for this hotel was greatly hindered by something called government sequestration. This is basically where the government cuts back significantly on spending. Overnight, a large portion of our fees for the year dried up. Not to mention two brand new Hilton flags opened in our market that same year as well. They stole market share from our full-service Hilton branded property. All our Washington, DC, area hotels that we had under management were under budget in fees to the amount of approximately $200,000 collectively. Just that Hilton property alone represented approximately $150,000 of that deficit. Because of God's provision in that year, those fourteen properties that came onboard supplied enough fees to make up the difference and more. This allowed for little disruption to our corporate team as well as our staffing.

I prayed for ten hotels, but God knew we needed more to supply for the needs of our company. He knows exactly what we need, and nothing is too difficult or large for Him to accomplish. God honors big bold prayers. He is inviting us to ask. Jesus told his friends this in Matthew 7:7–8, "Ask, and it will be given to you. Seek, and you will find. Knock, and the door will be opened to you. For everyone who asks receives, and the one who seeks finds, and to the one who knocks, the door will be opened." If you have not received an answer yet, continue to keep seeking and knocking. Don't give up on yourself. Don't give up on God.

You know if you have been sales for some time that the answer is always "no" unless you ask. God is inviting us to keep asking. One of the best sales, leadership, and life tools you and I can ever tap into is the power of prayer. Prayer helps you accomplish a lot:

- It's an opportunity to connect with the God of the universe, who desires a relationship with you.
- It's an opportunity to present requests, challenges, burdens, and praises—not just on behalf of ourselves but also on behalf of others.
- It's an opportunity to pray for others, which combats looking inward and helps us focus outward.
- It helps provide wisdom and clarity with situations we may be facing—not just for ourselves personally but also for our team, which may include our family or work family.
- It takes the pressure off us, forcing circumstances and outcomes to happen, and gives things back to God to do what only He can do.
- It's an opportunity to pray prayers that will outlast us long after we are gone.

Simply put, prayer changes things. Mainly ourselves.

You Can Connect with Great People

In recent years I have frequently prayed that God would connect me, our family, and our company to great people. I may as well have circled this one. I pray for this ultimately so that at the end of the day, the kingdom of heaven can see the most benefit. However, from a business development standpoint, when God answers this prayer, I see our team and people benefit as well. When we work or partner with great individuals, our work environment becomes even better. From a personal and family perspective we benefit because life is a lot more fun when you are working alongside amazing individuals.

This prayer has been interesting to see God answer on a regular basis. I smile often as conversations develop with prospective clients. I hear and see how people get connected to me and our company through unique circumstances. Something about our corporate culture, values, and connection to God stands out to them.

One day shortly after starting to pray this prayer, I reached out to a prospective group about a project in Ohio. I left a message and sent a follow up email. It did not take long to receive a call back from the principal of the firm. My inquiry got his attention, and he wanted to learn more about our company. We talked for a little while and at the end of the conversation, he said what stood out to him was how similar our values were. Sure enough, I went back through their website after the discussion and saw how God was an important part of their company. I do not know how I missed it before.

Just because it hasn't rained yet doesn't mean we stop praying. One of the greatest lessons we can learn as we grow and mature in our walk with God is trusting Him no matter what happens. If God is for you, who can be against you? If God is for you, then He knows exactly what is needed to help you achieve the greatest level of success.

Author and speaker Bob Goff said, "Hope doesn't go to sleep because it's dark outside. It lights a candle and stays up, waiting for the rest of the story. Are you living in anticipation of God surprising you? This is the place where God meets us. He finds us in the places between the miracles."

Keep praying. Keep believing. Keep hoping.

Don't give up on yourself. Don't give up on God. He's not giving up on you.

A Different Point of View

How God answered the prayer I circled in 2013 changed the way I have looked at selling from that point onward. I have been in countless selling situations since then, working with our team to acquire new business for the company. Many of these opportunities require a lot of time and effort. Many more of them simply do not come to fruition. While I always want to win (as you do, I am sure), I try acknowledging that if we don't, it is because God is protecting me and you from a business relationship that we do not need to be a part of.

Relationships are not perfect. When people work with people, it is only a matter of time before disagreements and differences of opinion cause friction. The more closely aligned you can be with another group or person in terms of values and understanding, the greater chance you have of that relationship being successful. Difficult circumstances will come, and it is how we collectively navigate them together as human beings that will determine whether we will make it through.

Because I know God is for me, I do not worry if a deal does not go through or not. I trust that He knows what is best for our business and myself. I am praying that He will build the bridges to the right relationships and projects. The challenge is to remain patient and steadfast while both are being built.

As a salesperson you can gain valuable learning lessons in the deals you lose just as much as the ones you gain. Harvest as much knowledge as you can from the sales situations you fail in and use what you have learned on the road ahead. Move ahead without fear and lead with confidence knowing that God has your back no matter what.

Another Note on the Hilton

Our Hilton team was an excellent one. Another miraculous thing that happened in 2013 was that the brand was considering pulling us out of the system or pushing us to another Hilton franchise. Because of our teams' efforts, we were able to avert Hilton's dropping the franchise at the hotel, which would in turn make us switch to another brand at the property. Having to change your flag (hotel franchise) on a hotel building always hurts business for a while. It can cost a hotel location millions of dollars. Our property had been a Hilton for thirty years. Having Hilton extend the franchise at our property for another fifteen-to-twenty years was miraculous.

Unfortunately, the property did not fully recover from government sequestration and struggled for a long time afterward. Finally, thinking we would have a breakout year and see significant improvements, the year was 2020. And after a solid initial start, everything fell apart beginning in March of 2020. We ultimately ended up losing this property. While we miss the hotel and our hotel family dearly, God had other plans for us. Remember He knows what is best and what exactly is needed to succeed. Just because something may look hopeless on the surface does not mean that God does not have something amazing planned on the other side.

Ideas

Always ask for the business. The answer is always a guaranteed "no" unless you do. Potential bridges to opportunities are to always greet and introduce yourself to people regardless of the situation.

I often went to places with my grandfather. He always would say hello to the people sitting beside him wherever we went, even at a Broadway play. He eventually turned to me and said it is always a good idea to get to know the people around you. He was right, you never know who you will meet. Plus, it is always better to sit next to a new friend versus a stranger. Take time to say hello.

Questions to Consider

- Sometimes you, your company, or specific department need to evaluate performance. You need to assess your strengths and weaknesses. You need to brainstorm, strategize, and review how you can be better for your customers. You can pray through all things that are faced.

- When thinking about your company or a dream or idea you are looking to sell, what do you and your team want collectively to
    1. Start doing?
    2. Stop doing?
    3. Keep doing?
- What is a bold prayer you can start circling and praying to God for today?

Our aim is to produce such genuinely good, solid, and decent work that people must always acknowledge that LEGO makes quality products. My prayer to the Lord for LEGO is that he will help us run a business that is honest in every way, in our life and dealings, so that our actions and our lives are lived in his honor and with his blessing.

—Ole Kirk Christiansen, Billund, Denmark, June 19, 1942

Your Takeaways

What is a takeaway for you in this chapter? What do you want to remember and come back to again for encouragement and inspiration? Seek to write out some of those thoughts here:

___

___

___

___

___

___

___

___

___

___

___

CHAPTER 10

From Here to There: Getting from A to B

The greatest use of life is to spend it for something that outlasts it.
—William James

We are all in positions where we are trying to get from one place to another as best as we possibly can. This starts from the moment we're born. As children we immediately go through different stages of life, learning and growing. Many take the same pathway pattern from standing, to walking, to talking, and on to running and bruising our legs on the playground. We move into elementary school and rise from kindergarten to first grade. As we get older, the hurdle points in between the next *A* to *B* get more complicated and challenging. We are all progressively moving from one place to the next in things like

- Moving through school toward graduation.
- Graduating and then on to a new job and career.
- Single to being married.
- Gaining new friendships and relationships.
- Learning a new skill or enhancing existing ones.
- From sickness to health.
- Achievement in any form, like winning a game, trophy, or new contract.
- Saving money, investing correctly, and building wealth.
- Getting out of a mess or difficult situation whether it was our own fault or not.
- Indecision to decision.
- Discomfort to contentment and peace.

Regression on any of the above is another route we can go, but I do not believe most people want to move backward. If we are going to be effective at selling in life, the way we approach getting from one point to another is important. We will never completely avoid mistakes as we approach and go past these hurdle points. In fact, we should embrace them when they occur because they help us learn and grow. Legendary UCLA basketball coach John Wooden said, "If you are not making mistakes, then you are not doing anything. I'm positive that a doer makes mistakes."[1] Building a strong foundation around our decision-making ability will help us to take steps forward on a ground that is surer and steadier beneath our feet. So, how do we get from the A's to B's in our life as best as we possibly can?

The Little Miracle of A *to* B

The Bible provides us with incredible lessons on leadership and effective living that are applicable today just as they were centuries ago. A story in the Gospel of John might give us insight into this. Embedded within this story is reference to a miracle that you may not have caught before. Over the years I have read this story many times and completely missed it myself. I believe it gives us a great picture of what is needed so that God can start doing what only He can do in and through us. Before we get to this miracle though, we read about another famous miracle first.

Jesus and his disciples had been on the western side of the Sea of Galilee, where He was speaking and preaching to thousands of people who were far from home. They were all hungry, so out of compassion he miraculously fed all 5000 of them. After that incredible miracle of provision, Jesus told his disciples to go ahead of Him as He took a little time for himself to rest and pray.

Here is a sidebar question, how many of us in seasons of busyness take time to rest and recuperate? Do we build any time at all to detach and decompress? This is a lesson that Jesus demonstrates a lot over the course of His ministry on earth. If we go full throttle all the time, we are not going to be as effective at life whether we are selling or otherwise. One of my greatest weaknesses and perhaps yours as well, is the ability to be still.

Back to John's story, picking up in verse 18. A *high wind arose*, and the sea began to churn. After they had rowed about *three or four miles,* they saw Jesus walking on the sea. He was coming near the boat, and *they were afraid* (John 6:18–19, emphasis added).

The Sea of Galilee is about seven miles by twelve miles. If they had been rowing three or four miles from Tiberias, the group would have been right in the middle of the lake. They were most likely worn out from a full day and rowing together for hours. This area is prone to unpredictable weather, and the rough seas were not helping them at all. And because it was in the early morning hours, there was hardly any light besides maybe distant lamps they could probably barely see anyway.

They were fearful about all the signs and circumstances around them. Even though they were together, they were afraid of what the next moment would bring. "But he said to them, 'It is I. Don't be afraid.' Then they were willing to take him on board, and *at once the boat was at the shore where they were heading*" (John 6:20–21, emphasis added).

The easily recognizable miracle is Jesus' walking on the water to his friends in a stormy sea. The less recognizable one is when they invited Jesus on board the boat, they immediately reached the shore where they were going. That's amazing! Thirteen guys and a boat were just whisked over to the shore where they needed to go. While we might not be able to do that with a boat, there are action steps we can take from this story to help us effectively get from our next A to the shore of our next B.

Do you ever feel that when you're trying to get from one place to the next, you become tired and worn out? You may feel stuck in the middle of the situation you are in without any movement forward. I have been there before. Typically, I am not one to give up. I will push through as best I can and keep fighting and struggling. When I have forced circumstances to happen, I thought made sense, it has usually not worked out very well in my favor. Ultimately, I end up where I do not really want to be. More importantly, I do not end up where God wants me to be.

It does not always have to be negative roads we walk down that become the ones we should get off. Over the years, I have taken time to receive a master's degree, a brokerage pre-license certification, and have I've been licensed to do foster care. I have signed up for committees, advisory boards, and other commitments that are all good things to be a part of. However, several of them slammed back in my face. They were situations I willingly signed up for but ultimately needed to end.

Even what may seem like good, calm water initially can change into rough seas out of nowhere, causing fatigue, frustration, and distraction. We need discernment to help us determine the best way to spend our most important asset, which is time. If we allocate too much of it away from what is truly important, we will have a harder time rowing from our present *A* location to our preferred *B* destination.

As we face hurdles in life, a lot of emotions can arise. We become worried about getting our next paycheck, hitting our benchmarks, and meeting expectations from those around us. On Sundays we may become fearful about what Monday and the rest of the week will bring. The disciples were right there as well.

Recognize God for Who He Is

In the book of Exodus, Moses encounters a miraculous moment with God in the form of a burning bush. In the exchange, God tells Moses about what He wants him to do and where He wants him to go. This was a big *A* to *B* situation. God tells Moses to go back and talk to Pharaoh in Egypt and to tell the man that the Israelites need to be let go. Moses, like we probably would be, was fearful and doubtful in himself. He asks God a question. What should he tell everyone if they ask who is sending him there to tell everyone the wonderful news. God said to Moses, "I AM that I AM." And He said, "You must say this to the Israelites, 'I AM has sent me to you.'" Exodus 3:14). It's like Jesus calling out to us in the middle of where we are and where we are trying to go. "Hey, it's me! I AM right here!"

Sometimes it takes God reminding us of who He is. In John's gospel he notes several statements Jesus makes about himself. An example of this is in chapter 10 verse 11, where Jesus says, "I am the good shepherd. The good shepherd lays down his life for the sheep." It is in our moments of doubt, fear, concern, and frustrations when we need to focus on who He is and how He sees us. Too often we focus on how we see ourselves. When we do this, we are certainly going to have doubts and be fearful along our path from *A* to *B*.

When I was thirty-four years old, I moved into the CEO position for our company. The year was 2017. Up until that point I had been working in a business development role for many years. I was excited to go from this *A* to *B* point in this next stage of my life, but I was also nervous about the unknown. Nothing can quite prepare you for certain sales or leadership positions until you have stepped into them with both feet. It is kind of like becoming a parent. There is no book or tutorial lesson that can completely prepare you for having children. While our business was based in Maryland, I had been living in Central Florida for about nine years. There were countless times I traveled down from Volusia County to the Orlando airport. I would fly from Orlando to Baltimore and drive from Baltimore to our office in Maryland near DC. The trip took around six hours if there were no delays. Typically, weather, mechanical issues, or other circumstances would cause some kind of delay. Looking back, I do not know how I did it for as long as I did.

One early morning, I was driving to the Orlando airport, thinking about the upcoming leadership transition. My thoughts drifted to the story of David when he was becoming king of Israel. I thought there was no way he could have felt like he was ready to be king. I started saying to God that I did not think I was ready to take on this large role and be CEO. In one of the very few times in my life where I felt God audibly speak to me, I felt Him say, "You're not, but I am."

If we want to be successful while getting from *A* to *B*, we need to submit ourselves under the acknowledgement and truth that He is God, and we are not. Where and when we feel incapable, He can get us to and through any situation we face. He can help us be a better leader and salesperson than we could ever achieve totally on our own. God was right. I was not ready for what I was about to face in the weeks, months, and years ahead. Suffice to say, I am glad I had Him to turn to.

Don't Be Afraid of Where You Are Currently or Where You Are Going

When Jesus walks on the water toward the fishing boat, the first thing he says to his frightened disciples is essentially, "Hey guys it's me!" Notice it was not the other way around. Typically, when people tell us not to panic or be afraid, that is exactly what we do. He wanted his disciples to know it was Him. In fact, in all three versions of this story from the other Gospel accounts Jesus tells them it is Him before saying do not be afraid. Why does He do this? I think it is because God wants you to know that He is with you no matter what. When you hear and recognize the presence of your loving heavenly Father, it gives you the strength of heart to keep pressing forward.

Being scared seems to be more temporary and fleeting. However, fear is rough and feels deep-seated. If you let it take over, it can rob you of your joy. When it comes to selling and developing your character, fear has the propensity to steal your future hopes and dreams. Most importantly it can keep you from the *A* to the next *B* path that God has planned for you.

This happened in the Book of Numbers. The Israelites had made it through the desert and had approached the Promised Land. Twelve scouts were sent ahead to explore and report back to the nation the entire good and bad about the situation they were entering. All but two of them (Caleb and Joshua) came back in a panic about the size and appearance of strength the people of the land possessed. Joshua and Caleb said to the people in Numbers 14:9, "Don't be afraid of the people of the land, for we will devour them. Their protection has been removed from them, and the LORD is with us. Don't be afraid of them!"

Despite all that they had seen and experienced with God being there for them and keeping His promises, they became fearful. The group of people wanted to stone Joshua and Caleb for their confident words. This response of fearfulness cost the nation of Israel another forty years wandering around in the desert. A whole generation passed away before the next could enter the Promised Land.

When you become fearful of what may be ahead, remember God's promises. The author of Hebrews writes in chapter 13 verse 6: "The Lord is my helper; I will not be afraid. What can man do to me?"

What does this tell us? If the next action or step that you feel called to take is causing anxiety or fear, ask yourself why—especially knowing that God is on your side.

Reach out if someone is on your mind.

Be willing to forgive.

Give without expecting anything back.

Try even though you may fail.

Take the next step from A to B even though you may not know where that step will lead.

What are you afraid of really?

Who are you afraid of really?

Get God into Your Boat

It was only until the disciples invited Jesus into the boat that they were able reach the shore of where they wanted to be. The boat is a good representation of our life. God is not going to just climb in. We must invite Him. He wants us to be the ones to invite Him to come aboard. When we do that, we soon recognize that it is His boat after all, and we can thankfully pass the oars or wheel over to Him. It does not necessarily mean the seas around us will be any less choppy. However, we can be confident knowing that we are headed in the right direction, and we will not sink no matter what.

When our kids were younger, my wife, Stephanie, and I felt that we needed to move. We loved living where we were in Florida. We had great friends and neighbors. We had wonderful memories and family that were not far away. However, something kept jabbing at us that we needed to be somewhere else by the time our older son turned ten. We had no idea where that was supposed to be, only that we needed to get there.

We started praying and created a basic list of what we desired the next place would have. A preeminent focal point for us was not what we wanted for ourselves, but what would be best for our kids. If you want to be successful at selling and getting from *A* to *B*, you shouldn't just look inward. You should also look outward at what you can do for others. Again, we had no idea where we were supposed to be. As it would happen, circumstances took us through central North Carolina. We did some initial brief research on the central North Carolina area and decided to make the move.

I would have never imagined living where we are now, but it has become our favorite place. God has provided more than we could ever have imagined. We had even clipped a picture from a magazine of a future home we hoped for. When I pulled up into our neighborhood the first time, the house looked so like the picture we had clipped. We were amazed and thankful. I believe when your priorities align with God's promises and desires you can never go wrong.

I am so thankful that years ago I invited Jesus into my lifeboat. It does not mean that the paths I have taken have been easy. They have been quite difficult. It does not mean I have not been fearful. I have had many sleepless nights, thinking about what the day ahead may bring. Yet when you walk forward in faith, trusting in His promises, you can never truly fail. God will work all things out for good no matter what.

If you have never asked Him to get into your boat, you can do that right now. Just stop, pray, and ask Him to climb aboard. Perhaps you already have Jesus in your boat, but you have been trying to row on your own for too long. Now is the time to let Him steer the ship. In both cases when we make the decision to invite God in and take control, we will be better for it. Psalm 51:12 says, "Restore the joy of your salvation to me, and sustain me by giving me a willing spirit." Be willing to make the invitation and hand over the oars.

You will never regret it.

When the Ride Is Rough to Point B

Remember getting to the shore is just the beginning. You may not be able to go back once you have arrived, but you can always remember back.

You can remember how God brought and carried you through all kinds of circumstances to your current destination. From where you were to where you are and ultimately where you want to be.

Before I became CEO, we went through a challenging season. My wife was dealing with some health issues that she had finally got behind her. Three days after I transitioned into the new leadership role, we were in a home improvement store. We were in the garden center on a Saturday, and Stephanie said she would go to the car while I wrapped things up. She took both of our boys with her while I went inside the store and grabbed a couple more items. When I got back into the garden center area, I thought I had heard my name over the loudspeaker. No way, it couldn't be me.

I then got a phone call. The person on the other end said that I needed to come out to the parking lot right away. I dropped everything, ran outside, and saw my wife on the ground. A vehicle had hit her, and the tire stopped on her left foot. Any vehicle would be bad, but this being a huge SUV, made it one of the worst ones possible! Thank God the vehicle narrowly missed hitting our younger son. Unfortunately for my wife, we found out that the metatarsals in the arch of her foot had been fractured. The person who stopped on her foot just did not see her. Ironically, the guy was an ophthalmologist.

The days that followed were difficult for Stephanie and our family. Beyond the new job and fractured foot, our dog was dying of tongue cancer. Then one night while I was away, I got a call from Stephanie that someone was trying to break into the house. It turned out to be a contact whom we knew through a neighbor who lived in a development down the street. Some days later this same person's wife put mail in our box stating bad comments about us. None of the comments were true. Weeks later, this same guy held his wife and child at gunpoint while the police came and arrested him. It was a wild season.

Stephanie and I were trying to take our family from where we had been into a new season of life. We were aiming to be in a new position with me as CEO and her in full health, along with co-teaching our kids. We wonder why we must go through these rocky, turbulent seas sometimes. It is because God wants us to turn to Him, recognize who is He, and let Him take the oars. I would not trade those experiences for anything because I believe they helped accomplish at least three things:

1. They helped me and our family become more resilient and stronger for greater challenges that would lie ahead, particularly leading and taking our company through the pandemic.
2. They cultivated in us a greater ability to be empathetic toward others going through difficult situations.
3. They helped strengthen our character; the traits we want to grow and develop in us.

If you want to be successful at selling yourself in life, you must be able to get down on the same level with people. A great character trait that is worth its weight in gold is the ability to show empathy. Bob Iger, who was the President and CEO of Disney for fifteen plus years, took the company through major acquisitions and partnerships. In his book, *Ride of Lifetime*, Iger writes, "Over the next few years, as we made the major acquisitions that redefined and revitalized our company, this simple, seemingly trite, idea was as important as all of the data-crunching in the world: If you approach and engage people with respect and empathy, the seemingly impossible can become real."[2]

I think the impossible *can* become real when you are truly real with others. The demonstration of genuine care and concern for others stands out in a sea of sameness. Becoming known as a great listener and encourager makes you memorable. Everything combined, if done correctly, will hopefully leave an impression that will last well beyond your days.

Ideas

Maximize Your Time

There are great ways you can maximize your time while driving or travelling from one place to the next. One of the things I like to do is batch together my calls. This means what I will do is make a list of all the people and prospects I need to call. I call them one after the other while I'm driving.

After I have completed my calls, I will find a podcast or some type of audio message I can listen to. Many speakers in the past have given these different names. I think it is safe to refer to it as the "Driving University." You are taking what would otherwise be unused time and channeling it into moments where you can learn and grow.

Embrace the Cold Call

Embrace the cold call, or unsolicited introductory call. It has become a lost art. What are you afraid of really if the person on the other end doesn't call back or tells you, "No thanks"? Make a call or visit now that you have been avoiding out of fear. Write down the results of that call.

Questions to Consider

- Where are you now? What is your current *A* situation?
- What *B* are you moving toward? What is the shore you are trying to reach next?
- What do you think we typically fear most?
- Who do you have in your boat?

Determine that the thing can and shall be done
and then we shall find the way.
—Abraham Lincoln

Your Takeaways

Based on what you read in this chapter, what are some action steps you want to begin taking now to get from your current *A* to your next *B* destination? Take a moment to write out some of those thoughts here.

CHAPTER 11

Leadership

To a young man who has in himself the magnificent possibilities of life, it is not fit that he should be permanently commanded. He should be a commander.
—James Garfield

The Republican National Convention was already passing through its fourth day on June 6, 1880. James Garfield made his way to the Interstate Industrial Exposition Building. It was a beautiful structure that had risen from the ashes of the great Chicago Fire of 1871. The city, streets, and hotels were packed with people. Garfield himself was getting little sleep due to sharing a bed with someone he did not know. Delegates were split for different candidates. Among them was Ulysses S. Grant, going for a third term. James Garfield was supporting James Sherman (brother of William Tecumseh Sherman). He did not believe Sherman was the best candidate but felt an obligation to give a speech about him. Garfield had become an eloquent speaker over the years, and as he was concluding his speech, he looked out over the crowd and said, "And now, gentlemen of the Convention, what do we want?" From the crowd came a surprising response, "We want Garfield!"[1] A speech that had been intended to promote Sherman became more compelling at that moment for Garfield himself.

Stepping back further in time from this moment, we know that Garfield's life was anything but easy. His father died at the early age of thirty-three, leaving his family in rural Ohio with little money or opportunity. They literally had nothing. Garfield didn't have a pair of shoes until he was four years old. But his mother believed in him and begged her second son to get a good education. Despite her pleas, James left home at the age of sixteen to work on the Erie and Ohio Canal. It was not until narrowly escaping a drowning incident that James came back home. In reflection he stated, "I did not believe that God had paid any attention to me on my account, but I thought He had saved me for my mother and something greater and better than canaling."[2] He ended up taking what little money that could be afforded and started attending a preparatory school in northern Ohio called the Western Reserve Eclectic Institute. Garfield's path of education moved quickly as he eventually attended Williams College in Massachusetts. He then made his way back to the Institute, and by the age of twenty-six had become the school's president. Amid his time in academics, James stated, "I am resolved to make a mark in the world. There is some slumbering thunder in my soul, and it shall come out."[3]

Later Garfield moved into politics only to be thrust shortly thereafter into the American Civil War. Despite having no prior military background or knowledge, Garfield eventually earned the rank of major general. At the conclusion of the war, he again served in Congress for many years. After all that time of leading and growing, Garfield found himself on stage at the convention in 1880, hearing that people wanted him to be president. It was unexpected, and it was not something that James desired in the slightest. Regardless of how he felt, Garfield went on to win the nomination and eventually became the twentieth President of the United States of America.

I think about James Garfield's story and everything that led up to that moment. Not all of us desire necessarily to be placed in positions of leadership. Yet due to our character, who we are, and where we have been placed, there is a call upon our lives to lead. Sometimes it's verbally requested, but most of the time it is nonverbally desired. The world needs great leaders. That world may not be oceans or states away. It extends much closer from your home to the other porches in the community and neighborhood around you. Whether stated or not, people desire and are drawn to solid leaders.

Good leadership, while less related to selling specifically, is an important thread that binds our character together. Without it, we will only go so far in our pursuit of selling ourselves well. We are all leaders because we all have influence in our people's lives. However, the influence we extend can go in the direction of being good or bad. The trick is growing and emulating the good traits versus the bad.

This book wasn't intended to be a book on leadership. However, at some point there will be someone in your life who needs you to be a leader. This could be a friend, spouse, daughter, son, or some other relative. It could be a co-worker, a team member, or some random bystander you have never met. When I became CEO, it was just a leadership title. I had been a leader way before my position changed. So have you. The following are some quick lessons I have learned on leadership. My hope is that when people most need you to take the lead, which could be daily for some, these lessons will be helpful for you.

Finish the Race

So often when people know that their time is coming to an end on a project, assignment, or contract they tend to give less than 100 percent.

People start to show up late, their quality of work declines, they don't care as much, and they begin to simply go through the motions. Often when our hotel management projects are set to be terminated, we typically have a thirty-to-ninety-day period before handing the asset over to another management company. I have always said to those I work with to make sure they finish the race.

When we seek to finish the race, no matter how many steps of time remain in the contract, agreement, task, or assignment, we should seek to cross the finish line as strong as we can. We don't want to allow anyone to say we dropped the ball or left something on the table. It's an opportunity for us to do our very best to the end.

Strength and Confidence

My cousin, Jim, had worked for our company since he was eighteen years old. I worked underneath him as a teenager when he was General Manager at a Holiday Inn our family owned. He eventually went on to become one of our Vice President of Operations. Every Monday for years we had a leadership call where everyone would provide updates for their roles and departments for the week. One Monday Jim came on the line and gave his update; everyone gave theirs, and we wrapped up the call as we normally did. Later that afternoon I got a call that Jim had passed away. We think he had a heart attack and never woke up.

This was devastating. Not only was Jim family, but we had also worked closely together for many years. It's times like this when you want to take time to remove yourself from people and process big questions. However, when it comes to leadership, this is just not something you can do. It is in difficult, challenging moments that leaders are needed the most. They are needed to provide strength and confidence to everyone else. So, what did I do?

As VP of Operations, Jim directly oversaw several hotels whose clients relied strongly on that oversight. He also worked closely with several general managers and associates who reported directly to him. The first thing I did before informing any of our clients or general managers was to forge a game plan with our executive team for who would be overseeing his properties. Once we had that game plan in place, I called each of Jim's owners and explained what had happened and who would be providing oversight into their location. I did the same thing with all the general managers. It was a lot of communication in a short amount of time, and there were also a lot of tears.

As painful as it was to do, everything we did aimed to leave no room for confusion or doubt. I have seen leadership transitions done improperly, and the outcome is quite the opposite. What you get is a bunch of frustration, concern, fears, doubts, and so on. In both the hard circumstances and good ones, people need you to be a strong leader. Doing so embeds confidence. It gives others the heart to continue moving forward, stay focused, and give their best. Losing Jim was incredibly sad and left a void. We lost a cousin, a dad, a friend, and colleague. We did not, however, lose the oversight, performance, and results that Jim worked so hard daily to build.

Set the Example

Over the years we have worked for many great clients. However, there have been some who have not set the best example for those that have worked for them. We can learn a lot from the good leaders we work for and equally a lot from the bad leaders. I believe we all want to display the types of leadership traits we want others to replicate rather than avoid.

We had one owner who only cared about their work and their hotels. They had a closer working relationship with Jim and even came to this funeral. I'll never forget standing at one side of the funeral home, looking across the room, and seeing this owner. He was having one of our accountants sign paperwork next to my cousin's casket. I'll never forget that image as long as I live. It is a reminder that work shouldn't always be the priority. There are times and places for everything. People should take precedence.

Another client we worked for had an incredibly successful hotel. They tended to layer on guilt like you wouldn't believe. In one instance I was driving through New York and received a call from them later in the evening. I picked up the phone and said, "Good evening," in a happy cheery voice. They immediately started yelling at me. It was so bad that I almost drove off the road. By the end of the one-sided conversation they said, "Wow me. I want to be wowed," then they hung up. It was basically them saying to me, "Dance, monkey, dance." That situation was a lesson to me to never be condescending or to berate and yell at others. Doing this to the people who work for you or those you are around doesn't get you far. It's more likely to push them away.

We once managed another property where the staff got together to celebrate birthdays for the month. The owner came in the break room and told everyone, "We don't celebrate." The general manager, who organized the time for everyone, had bought the cake with their own money. This was another case where profits were placed above people. It should be the other way around. When you put people above profits, then profits always come.

Here is a positive story. Earlier in the book I mentioned my time working at Disney's Polynesian Resort. I'll never forget working on Christmas Eve. We worked through the end of our shift at the restaurant later in the evening. I was walking out of the resort toward my car in the parking lot. The general manager of the resort was at the exit with his wife, greeting all the cast members who were leaving and offering them hot chocolate, a smile, and words of appreciation. They will never remember me, but that kindness left a great impression I'll never forget. We as leaders can leave a lasting impression on others. Let's seek to make it positive.

Serve, Pray, Encourage

I have said in this book that one of our values of an organization has been that the greatest leaders are the greatest servants. As leaders we should be the first to raise a hand to serve and get ourselves in the game. This is not saying to be a goody two shoes, holier than thou, or a suck-up. If people see that in you, then it's too bad. Rather, simply approach the situations you are placed in and look for ways to be of service. When you consistently seek to be the first to raise a hand, then I guarantee you will stand out.

Sometimes this can be recognizing moments for what they are and leading and encouraging when the other person needs it. Over the years I have been in different conversations when managers were experiencing challenging circumstances. Loved ones were in the hospital, or they themselves were dealing with difficult health conditions. I was on the phone with a manager who was driving to the scene of an accident that his son was involved in. I could have said just keep us posted and gotten off the call. No, I took the time to pray for him in that moment and encourage letting him know that God had everything under control. He did. And his son ended up being okay.

As leaders, one of our foremost responsibilities is to encourage those around us. My son has been on the cross-country team at his school. It is a group of amazing young leaders. However, there are always a couple here and there who need to grow a little more. One of his teammates has said after several races, "Hey, I beat you!" That's the opposite of being a leader and a team player. That's trying to lift oneself up by putting others down. It never works.

No matter how high a position you climb to, no matter how good you get at a particular skill, and no matter how big you grow your organization, remember this: Don't grow beyond your capacity to care. When you have exceeded that threshold, then you are not winning anymore.

Ideas

Bring Solutions with Problems

When it comes to business and life, there will never be a shortage of problems and issues to address. Typically, what happens is that most people bring along complaints and problems for the leader to address. They put it in someone else's lap to figure out and deal with. If you want to stand out and be different from the rest, then bring possible solutions along with the problems you highlight. Here is an example of a good way to think and speak: "I wanted you to know that we are seeing communication issues in our department. I have thought about it, and one of the ways I think this could be improved is if we had a weekly touch-base collectively as a team."

Along with this it is important to not finger point and complain if you haven't experienced something for yourself. You could say that another department in the company doesn't get it. However, have you ever spent time trying to put yourself in those people's shoes? Leaders bring solutions, seek answers, and take time to understand the whole picture versus complain and point away from themselves.

Close the Loop or the Loop Will Close on You

This idea goes along with finishing the race. Quite often circumstances will be left unresolved. This could be a conversation that needs to be had but is avoided due to discomfort or awkwardness. Or it could be a provision of an agreement or contract that needs to be finalized or followed up. We have often said that things tend to grow tentacles or loops. Left unchecked, these loops or tentacles have the opportunity to get tangled and wrapped around future circumstances. Have the courage and persistence to close the loops on open-ended items. Otherwise, at some point in time the loops could close in on you.

Following Through on What You Say

This isn't so much of an idea versus just a good practical piece of advice. Remember that following through with the small statements is just important as with the large ones. If you can't be consistent and dependable in the small things, it will affect the large as well. Obviously, there are always exceptions and circumstances beyond your control. However, if you say that you will call, write, or be somewhere within a certain time, then do it. Dependability builds trust, and trust helps you sell more than most.

Seasons of Yes and No

I have heard it said that our greatest weaknesses are our strengths stretched to the max. I feel that my strengths are persistence and determination. This has caused me to normally say yes to jumping onto the trip, committee, ongoing call, team, and so on. The problem is that when you say yes to too many things, your plate gets full. You cannot lead and be at your best when you have stretched yourself too thin. Just remember that it is okay in certain seasons of life to say no more than you say yes. Doing so will make you more effective among those you work with and serve.

Questions to Consider

- Who is someone you have worked for that has displayed bad leadership? What is it about them that makes you say that?
- Who is someone you have worked for that has displayed great leadership? What is it about them that makes you say that?
- What do you feel are your best leadership skills?
- What is one that you feel needs to be strengthened?

The demand for leadership always exceeds the supply.
—Unknown

Your Takeaways

There is a lot to unpack about leadership. Was there a story or an example that was shared in this chapter that stood out to you? What do you want to remember?

CHAPTER 12

Teamwork

There is something about achieving a goal as a team, at which time, the entire team gives back the success to an individual, which makes one feel all warm and fuzzy, no matter how cold it may be.
—Eric Alexander, *The Summit*

On May 25, 2001, at about 10 a.m. local time in Nepal, Eric Weihenmayer, took the final steps to reach the summit of Mount Everest. With those final steps, Weihenmayer became the first blind person to ascend to the top of the highest mountain in the world. This accomplishment landed him on the cover of *Time* Magazine as well as brought him many other accolades and recognitions. As amazing as this accomplishment was on its own, a total of five world records were broken that day. In addition to the first blind man to make it to the summit, along with him was the oldest man at age sixty-four, the largest team to reach the summit at a total of nineteen, the first American father and son, and the largest camera at twenty-five pounds. Not only did these teams have to make it to the top. Each of them also had to get back down!

When considering how these feats were successful, what can we point to? The obvious aspects are preparation, patience, and of course, teamwork. When it comes to selling and being successful in our careers and in life, a fundamental thread of importance is found within teamwork—the ability to be a team player. Eric Alexander, who was a part of the climbing team assisting with Weihenmayer's accent of Everest, said, "Success for me was doing the thing that was best for everyone else and stuffing my pride, which wanted to say I was responsible for their summit."[1]

Alexander's friend Weihenmayer made a similar comment, reflecting on a separate climbing expedition before Everest. Adelbert Ames conveyed a similar sentiment as well before stepping onto the battlefield. The behaviors and character traits we nurture now will translate into results we reap in the future. When approaching teamwork and collaboration with others, we must have the right mindset going in. This does not just happen overnight. We must diligently work at it. We may never be fully ready for all the variables that come our way when it comes to the dynamics of working around people. With teamwork, we need to mentally train and prepare ourselves to seek the best for the whole verses the one. Our unit, team, or group will always fare better when we focus less on ourselves. This is true in the business world and at home.

Teams You May Be On

There are many teams in life where we have no choice in terms of how we become a part of them. We get assigned by a teacher, we get recruited, or we join a company. Our coworkers are who they are. Then there are the teams we have more ability to choose. We are the leader, the hiring manager, or the captain, and we have more of a say about who gets hired. We can collaboratively determine who should be in the right seats for the bus. Finally, there can be a combination of both. We may not be able to choose what team we are on, but we can choose to be a team player with the one we've been assigned to. Companies and people change as time progresses. Are you staying consistent across those changes? Are you seeking to be the kind of team player you expect of others?

Remember that your team is not just your office co-workers. The teams we build around us are comprised of others whom we care about and connect with. These people would certainly include our nuclear family that may be made up of our spouse and children. They would also include extended family with our moms, dads, grandparents, aunts, and uncles. Your team could include neighbors, club members, mentors, teachers, pastors, or your church family. All these people are important extensions of your succeeding in life.

Solomon, who is sometimes said to have been the wisest person who ever lived, wrote that "Plans fail when there is no counsel, but with many advisers they succeed" (Proverbs 15:22). This was coming from someone whom others from across the known world came to seek counsel. What was he saying? We should seek guidance, direction, and counsel from those we trust. It is important in life that we have a team.

We will be more successful at selling ourselves, our company, and our ideas if we surround ourselves with wise counsel and trusted advisors. These individuals know you. They can help see things from the outside looking in that you might not be able to notice completely on your own. They bring different thoughts and perspectives to help round off the edges of your thought process. It is most likely that their desire is to see you succeed and be the best you can be. If they truly care, they want to see the best character traits grow within you. Sometimes that means they may need to give you some tough love. We want people to be honest. I certainly do. The truth hurts sometimes, but unless we hear it, how can we improve? We must be humbly willing to hear what people feel they need to share with us. Once we hear the good, bad, and ugly, then we can decide on a direction to take with what has been communicated.

We should always feel that we can go back to people we trust and ask for their advice and guidance. The individuals you confide in become a part of your life team.

In work environments, some of us, depending on our personality, may tend to take over and railroad others. But successful teams and team members are inclusive, not exclusive. They work together, sharpening each other's strengths while collectively compensating for each other's weaknesses.

We can and should have the ability to make it on our own. With selling in life there will be times where if something is going to happen, it will be because we took charge and made it so. I have found over the course of my time in business that you reach a point in selling a deal where you are less effective alone. You can be more successful by bringing together more members of the team. The saying goes that there is no *I* in team.

Team Integration

In 2016 we were looking to work with a group based in the Mid-Atlantic. Their portfolio was made of properties up and down the east coast, some high-quality assets. This group was not far from our backyard, and we knew that if we were able to start working with them, it would be a big deal for us. The opportunities this group was looking to have us manage were not in the best condition. However, they were bigger boxes and close by. Yet we were going up against some thick competition. We did what had worked before and what had certainly worked for Eric Weihenmayer's team. We were patient, we prepared, and we came together as a team.

The time finally arrived to present our company and services to the client. Rather than going in alone, a group of us met at a hotel near the prospective client. The hotel was across the street from their offices, and the room I stayed in the night before looked right down at their office floor. I felt as if I were in an action spy movie. The day of the meeting our team met me at the hotel, and we all reviewed the presentation we were to give. We had previously spent time discussing projections of how we thought the hotels could perform. We visited the hotels in person and put together our notes of how we felt we could improve operations. At one point, before we made our way to the meeting, all of us were on the balcony, looking at the client's office building. It really did feel like an action spy movie.

We walked across the street and into the meeting. It was a packed room. We had someone from our team representing each department. Team members from operations, sales and marketing, accounting, and human resources each got a chance to tell who they were and what they did for the hotels. It all worked great because the client got to directly see the people they would be working with on a regular basis. Questions were answered in real time, and I believe confidence was established from the beginning. Seeing the whole team share who they were, their tenure and expertise was compelling. We got the assignment and eventually started operating three hotels for this group.

Getting the opportunity, the deal, assignment, approval, or whatever, is just the beginning. The real work begins on day one of the job. In every case, particularly with hotels and hospitality, it takes a team to make a dream happen and be successful.

This is the second component of effective teams: how well you integrate with the team. Would you consider yourself to be a team player? Perhaps your definition may mean something different to you versus what it may mean for someone else.

To me, being a team player means that you become a servant leader. What does this mean? You may or may not have been given a defined leadership title. Let us say you have not. So even if you're not the president of a division, captain of a group, manager of a store, or head of a company, you still have a role to play. You are still part of the team. You can equip and encourage those you are working with. You can have their backs even though they may not have yours. You can pick up the slack and go the extra mile when others may be new or struggling. You can say, "Here I am. How can I help?" rather than internally under the shadow of your subconscious say, "What is the least amount I can do?" You can always step up and be a leader by serving those around you. This includes friends, family members, and others in your inner circle. How can all this be true? Because it's a mindset.

While we may not always be able to choose those on our team, we always have the choice to care for those who are on it.

Great teams are comprised of solid servant leaders. Great leaders are good at serving rather than being served. As Weihenmayer's team ascended the frosted slopes of Mount Everest, there were many points along the way where the group would be linked together. Weihenmayer would be crossing a crevasse over a ladder. His team members would be ringing a bell to provide a sense of direction, and they would be harnessed together. They would not have been successful if they had not been looking out for the best for each other.

Can you imagine how your team would change if everyone sought the best for each other? There is no doubt that it takes drivenness to get things done. At times you must take the wheel yourself to keep things moving. Yet if your drivenness takes you inward rather than outward, you will be less appealing.

The path from where you are to where you want to be will certainly be filled with challenges, setbacks, and uncertainty. Building and growing strong character traits within yourself involves difficulty. Yet surrounding yourself with great people and being great for others makes it a lot more bearable and a lot more possible to reach the shore.

Once you arrive at the shore, that is just the beginning. The journey ahead is far.

Do not go alone. It is more fun together with others anyway.

Sword and Shield

The group that we started working for at the beginning of this chapter was initially good, and we operated three of their locations. Then a couple members of their team turned out to be brutal. They didn't yell, scream, or curse, though I've worked with clients like that. And it wasn't because we were not good; they were just angry people. These individuals were heavy handed in their expectations, and they were condescending toward our accounting staff and our requirements.

The assets themselves we were managing were close to home, but they needed some significant capital improvements. We did our best for these locations, but in the end, we parted ways. The relationship ended amicably, and we would be happy to work with this group again. I was on the phone with another group that was taking over one of the locations. I will never forget hearing that company representative say that they "did not believe in revenue management." If you're in the hotel business, you will understand that this statement makes no sense at all.

This client we worked for was very difficult. As a team player and leader, it is important that you know when to be the sword and when to be the shield. I have said this a lot over the years. It simply means that you know your timing of when to protect and defend your fellow team members. There are times when, out of selflessness, you willingly step in and take the beating in place of someone else. By beating I mean verbal lashing, frustration, disappointment, and possibly anger. You need to be the shield. Then there are other times where you need to be the sword. You are on the offensive, defending the actions and results of what the collective team or team member produced. You know what is right and are battling against misconceptions and untruths.

Nothing will sell others on you personally like stepping into the ring of fire in place of another. The greatest salespeople should be the ones seeking to serve not to be served.

Ideas

Take Time to Celebrate

Make sure you take time to celebrate your wins as a team. So often over the course of my career in selling, we have not done a good job at this. We have landed some incredible opportunities only to casually acknowledge the achievement and just continue moving onward. On one of the biggest deals I was able to sign up, the contract was signed, and I honestly felt terrible afterward. I thought, "Shouldn't I feel elated with joy right now? This should not be what winning feels like." It was a long struggle to get the deal across the finish line, and I felt that when it finally happened the team did not really care.

I do want to note that while I was able to get the deal across the finish line, nothing fully happens without the support of the team behind you. Even if you think you are a team of one, you really are not. This is true if you have built that support system and inner circle around you.

Some see new deals as if they were just more work or a box to be checked. Please do not do this. New deals and opportunities are life giving to your psyche. They foster continued motivation, excitement, confidence, and positivity. They generate new open doors, next steps, and possibilities for the future. New deals are also the lifeblood for your business. Take time to celebrate the wins. A win does not have to be a new contract. It could be implementing a new process, system, or tool successfully. It could be an outstanding letter from a client or guest who provided raving reviews about what you did for them. So much of what we deal with has the propensity to be negative. You and your team will be thankful you paused and celebrated a collective achievement together.

See Beyond the Moment

This is less of an idea but rather something I have always tried to do. When I am working on a new deal, I always try to look beyond the moment. I see the faces of the people whose lives will be impacted in a good way. When contracts are signed, new jobs are created, and existing jobs are preserved. I see new pathways to dreams being realized for others. It's not just about money. Money and finances are good things, but they are not the main things in life. God gives us His money and gifts to steward during the time He has provided us on earth. He wants us to use this time, our talents, and treasure to see beyond the moment and store up what we can take to heaven. Philippians 2:4 says, "Everyone should look not to his own interests, but rather to the interests of others."

That is teamwork.

Sell the Team

Sometimes you must sell your team on an opportunity. I have talked about taking projects down the road a little so that we can see what is around the corner. Members of your team may not want to go down that road to begin with. You must help sell them on the potential positive outcomes of what may transpire. What you are pursuing could potentially be a dead end or total failure. However, what if it turned out to be great? What are the potential outcomes if what you are chasing was successful in the end? Communicate those positive potential outcomes to those going alongside you.

Questions to Consider

- Can you remember a time that you successfully completed a project or opportunity with a team?
- What was it about that experience that made it work so well?
- How about the opposite. Can you think of some teams you have been on that did not work well together?

- What was it about those teams that made the experience unsuccessful?
- Who would you say is on your personal life team?

Talent wins games, teamwork and
intelligence wins championships.
—Michael Jordan

Your Takeaways

Being a team player is essential to being successful at sales and life. What are some thoughts or actions items you want to remember here?

____

____

____

____

____

____

____

____

____

____

____

____

____

____

____

____

____

____

____

Final Thoughts

A contact I once knew told me that one of the hardest things we can do is fill up empty blank pages with words. It is true. With writing you are creating something out of nothing. With the growth of artificial intelligence, this has become more effortless. It is certainly easier if you are letting a program generate or spark ideas for you. To truly write from your heart and mind can be very difficult. Couple that with finding and dedicating undistracted time makes it even more challenging. Over the course of putting this book together, I have carved out time in bookstores, hotels, coffee shops, planes, back porches, and little cramped spots on the floor.

One of the most difficult aspects of putting this book together for me was getting outside my own head. Countless moments I found myself saying, "No one is going to read this," or "Don't bother." I think self-doubt is one of the bigger hurdles we face. We have a hard time selling ourselves to ourselves. We slip down the path of believing a lie that we are not good enough. The reality is that we are more than enough because of who we belong to.

When we are connected to God, and if we have Jesus in our lifeboat, then we have a new identity. We do not have to be identified by our past hurts and mistakes. We do not have to associate who we are with our struggles and sufferings. God sees us as His sons and daughters. We are fully known and loved by Him just as we are. He can use us just as we are to accomplish great things. We do not have to believe a lie that if we do something, it will not matter or make a difference. It does. He can take any number of loaves and fish we present before Him and make it multiply. We just need to be willing to surrender them.

Why take the time to put these pages together? I get the opportunity to meet and connect with a lot of great people. However, regardless of whether someone is great, everyone, no matter who they are, experiences peaks and valleys. Some feel that they can never get out of the valley. Depression and anxiety are always at high rates. According to the National Institute of Mental Health, in 2021 suicide was the eleventh leading cause of death in the United States.[1] For those between the ages of ten to thirty-four, it is ranked at number two and number three. According to the CDC, in 2022 there were 49,000 deaths due to suicide.[2] That equates to one death every eleven minutes. Self-doubt, hopelessness, disbelief in oneself, and succumbing to the lie that we are not good enough are destroyers of life, opportunity, and potential.

I believe that these stats are true and are probably getting worse. One Sunday in between church services, I was sitting in my car, writing the back cover to this book. I had the windows down when someone I'd never met before approached me. While typing on my computer, he asked if I was aware of any resources I could direct him to. I asked if he could be more specific about what kind of resources he was looking for. He said he was looking for spiritual/mental health counseling because he had been considering taking his life. I closed my computer, got out of the car, and had a longer conversation with him.

During our time together, he expressed that he felt he should be thankful. Yet despite knowing the good things he had in life, if a weapon were in his home, he knew he'd use it and be gone. I told him that the enemy wants nothing more than to get us away from the campfire of community and into isolation. He wants us to believe lies about ourselves that simply aren't true. I reminded this man about who he belongs to and that who he is matters, that he isn't alone and to get back around the campfire of others who love him.

I started writing this book with the intention of appealing to as many people as possible. As time went on, though, I realized that these pages were not for the many but for the few. If you, dear reader, have been encouraged to take a step in the right direction, strengthen your character, learn how to sell more effectively, or get back around the campfire away from isolation, then this book was for you.

Who you are matters.

What you do matters.

Do not give up on yourself.

Keep leading.

Keep selling.

Acknowledgments

First and foremost, I want to thank my parents for always believing in me and supporting me. I was able to gain a lot of experience and memories because of the many years being able to work with and for my dad. I am thankful for those experiences across the country with the amazing people I was able to work with. I am thankful to Glen and Teresa as well for their love and support. I am also thankful to all the love and support of my family that includes my sister, sisters-in-law, and brothers-in-laws. All the above have made up a great team!

I also want to thank the many people that I have had the opportunity to work with at Coakley & Williams Hotel Equities, and others throughout my time in the hospitality industry. Thank you for the opportunities to lead, serve, collaborate, and overcome challenges together.

Several people read drafts of *Character Sells* and offered feedback. Mike, you went above and beyond with your initial review and comments. I'm happy to write alongside you any day. Also, I'm thankful to the amazing Charlene, Greg, Parker, and Lauren. Lauren may have been one of the last to get the document but was the first to offer feedback.

I am appreciative of others who lent a helping hand to the completion of this work. Thanks to Peter Lundell for your review of these pages. You took this work through the fire, and I am very appreciative. Thanks also to Cheri Cowell and the team at EABooks. I was praying for answer to getting this book published and God put you in my path.

Thanks for Ash and Ever for being the two best kids a guy could ask for. Never forget that winning off the field is more important than winning on the field! Thanks to my wonderful wife Stephanie, with whom I have had the privilege of sharing life for almost twenty years now.

We are getting to a point where we will have spent more time together than apart. She is a light in the lives of many people. I'm fortunate that she is a part of mine.

Last, and most important, thanks to the Lord, without whom I do not know how I would have persevered. He truly is the way maker / miracle worker. I am thankful He threw a hook in me to get this book completed. The journey is not over, though. I look forward to what He has planned next and getting to that next *B* destination. Until then let us all continue to keep leading and selling.

I'd love to hear from you! Email me at:
mark@charactersells.com

Notes

Front matter

1. Definition of the word, Sell—Merriam-Webster Dictionary online: https://www.merriam-webster.com/dictionary/sell

Getting Started

1. Mark Twain, BrainyQuote, 2026, https://www.brainyquote.com/quotes/mark_twain_118964.

Chapter 1: What You Need

1. Steve Schussler with Marvin Karlins, *It's a Jungle in There: Inspiring Lessons, Hard Won Insights, and Other Acts of Entrepreneurial Daring, 2nd ed.* (Schussler Creative Institute Publication., 2019), 26.
2. Steve Gilliland, Steve Gilliland, 2026, https://stevegilliland.com.

Chapter 2: What You Don't Need

1. Gordon Ramsay, *Humble Pie* (Harper Collins Publishers, 2007), 189.

Chapter 3: Looking at Failure Differently

1. Tom Hopkins, *How to Master the Art of Selling*, *3rd* ed. (Champion Press, 2005), 132.

2 Peg Moline, "We're far more afraid of failure than ghosts: Here's how to stare it down," *Los Angeles Times*, 2015, https://www.latimes.com/health/la-he-scared-20151031-story.html

3. "Norwest 2018 CEO Journey Study," study by Norwest venture and growth equity firm, 2018.

4. Quoted in Zig Ziglar, *Ziglar on Selling: The Ultimate Handbook for the Complete Sales Professional* (Oliver Nelson Books, 1991).
5. Jeremy Cowart, The Purpose Hotel, https://www.jeremycowart.com/purpose.
6. Wayne Gretzky, personal interview with Bob McKenzie, *The Toronto Star*, 1983.
7. Jack Canfield, *The Success Principles: How to Get from Where You Are to Where You Want to Be* (Harper Collins, 2005), 114.
8. John Maxwell, recorded event, date unknown.

Chapter 4: Preparedness

1. James B. Stewart, "Matchmaker," *The New Yorker*, August 31, 2001, https://www.newyorker.com/magazine/2001/08/20/matchmaker-2.

Chapter 5: Confidence and Building Effectiveness

1. Quoted in Michael J. Megelsh, *Adelbert Ames, the Civil War, and the Creation of Modern America* (Kent State University Press, 2024), 125.
2. Quoted in Megelsh, *Adelbert Ames*, 58.
3. Quoted in Megelsh, *Adelbert Ames*, 129.
4. Quoted in Megelsh, *Adelbert Ames*, 96.
5. Phil Knight, *Shoe Dog: A Memoir by the Creator of Nike* (Scribner, 2016), 55–56.
6. Quoted in Megelsh, *Adelbert Ames*, 131.

Chapter 6: Perseverance

1. Neil Coakley, unpublished personal journal, no date.
2. Alex Honnold with David Roberts, *Alone on the Wall*, 2015 (Revised edition, Pan Books, 2019), 5.
3. David Goggins, *Can't Hurt Me: Master Your Mind and Defy the Odds* (Lionpress Publishers, 2018), 73.
4. Fred Williams, unpublished personal journal, no date.

Chapter 7: Communication and Building Relationships

1. David McCullough, *The Great Bridge: The Epic Story of the Building of the Brooklyn Bridge*, 1972 (Simon and Schuster, 2001), 39–40.
2. McCullough, *Great Bridge*, 28.
3. Ken Sutterfield, *The Power of an Encouraging Word—Planting Seeds of Kindness to Reap a World in Bloom* (New Leaf Press, 1997), 16.
4. Sutterfield, *Encouraging Word*, 74.
5. *Aladdin*, directed by Ron Clements and John Musker (Walt Disney Pictures, 1992).

Chapter 9: Circles

1. Quoted in Jens Andersen, *The Lego Story: How a Little Toy Sparked the World's Imagination* (HarperCollins, 2021), 56.
2. Mark Batterson, *The Circle Maker: Praying Circles around Your Biggest Dreams and Greatest Fears* (Zondervan Expanded Edition, 2016) 15.
3. Andy Stanley, Sunday Sermon, North Point Community Church, Alpharetta, Georgia, July 12, 2020, Surviving Covid: An Interview with Stuart and Kellee Hall
4. Bob Goff quote, Sunday Sermon, North Point Community Church, Alpharetta, Georgia, July 12, 2020, Surviving Covid: An Interview with Stuart and Kellee Hall
5. Quoted in Jens Andersen, *The Lego Story: How a Little Toy Sparked the World's Imagination* (Harper Collins, 2021, 62.

Chapter 10: From Here to There: Getting from A to B

1. John Wooden, Brainy Quote, 2026, https://www.brainyquote.com/quotes/john_wooden_386958.

2. Robert Iger, The *Ride of Lifetime: Lessons Learned from 15 Years as CEO of the Walt Disney Company* (Random House, 2019), 120.

Chapter 11: Leadership

1. Quoted in Candice Millard, *Destiny of the Republic: A Tale of Madness, Medicine, and the Murder of a President* (Doubleday, 2011), 40.
2. Quoted in Millard, *Destiny of the Republic*, 21.
3. Quoted in Millard, *Destiny of the Republic*, 23.

Chapter 12: Teamwork

1. Eric Alexander, *The Summit: Faith Beyond Everests Death Zone* (New Leaf Press, 2010), 45.
2. Eric Alexander, *The Summit*: *Faith Beyond Everests Death Zone* (New Leaf Press, 2012), 90

Final Thoughts

1. "Suicide," National Institute of Health, accessed February 17, 2026, https://www.nimh.nih.gov/health/statistics/suicide.
2. "Provisional Suicide Deaths in the United States, 2022," CDC Newsroom, August 10, 2023, https://www.cdc.gov/media/releases/2023/s0810-US-Suicide-Deaths-2022.html#:~:text=Today%2C%20CDC%20is%20releasing%20the,care%20available%20to%20all%20Americans."

About the Author

Mark Williams has been in the hospitality industry for more than twenty years after graduating from University of Central Florida's Rosen College of Hospitality Management. He has worked for the Walt Disney World Company, served in business development roles, and been CEO for his family business. Currently, Mark is a Senior Vice President of Business Development for Hotel Equities, one of the largest hotel management companies in the United States. He resides in North Carolina, with his wife, Stephanie, their two sons, and yellow lab, who believes everyone in the world exists to love her.

About the Author

[illegible]

www.ingramcontent.com/pod-product-compliance
Lightning Source LLC
LaVergne TN
LVHW010659110826
845149LV00014B/3156

* 9 7 8 1 9 6 6 3 8 2 8 1 2 *